Leading with Jesus

Ministry Outside the Walls of a Church

Jennifer Smith

Dedicated to my husband, David, and my sons, Isaiah and Spencer. You all inspire me in ways you will never fully understand or realize.

Copyright © 2019 Jennifer L. Smith

All rights reserved. No part of this book may be reproduced or used in any manner without written permission of the copyright owner except for the use of quotations in a book review or on social media.

ISBN: 9798628346518

"Unless otherwise indicated, all Scripture quotations are from The ESV® Bible (The Holy Bible, English Standard Version®), copyright © 2001 by Crossway, a publishing ministry of Good News Publishers. Used by permission. All rights reserved."

First paperback edition May 2020.

Cover artwork by Emily Garcia. Cover design and page layout by Dede Simmons.

www.sharingloveandlife.com

"*Leading With Jesus* will awaken you to your ministry calling outside the walls of the church, motivate you to be a better leader, and equip you with practical lessons to empower you to lead better than ever before. Jennifer shares her real life lessons of godly marketplace leadership from the trenches of a successful business. Leading With Jesus isn't leadership theory. It is real life experience shared with each reader like a conversation over a cup of coffee."

Bobby Gourley
Author, *Tactics*, and Lead Pastor of Christ Chapel

"*Leading With Jesus* speaks into the core of every business owner wanting to lead with integrity. As a business owner, I found Jennifer Smith's wisdom both empowering and on point. This book embodies deep and meaningful tools sure to equip, enrich, and empower business owners to lead strong while communicating Christ's heart."

LaTan Murphy
Author, *Courageous Women of the Bible*

"Jennifer's heart shines in *Leading With Jesus* because she is committed to serving Him in her every day life. Her teachings are applicable for meaningful spiritual growth in the Christian life. Her real life experiences are compelling, inspirational, and authentic. There's also an undertone of quirkiness that makes you want to be her best friend. Jennifer is unique and kind— like an old retired pastor who can win most anyone to Jesus just by telling their testimony and somehow doing it in a way you'll remember forever."

Rachel Wammack
Singer/Songwriter, Sony Music

Table of Contents

Acknowledgments 9

Foreword 11

Chapter One | Finding the Why 13

Chapter Two | Jesus in the Marketplace: The Basics 25

Chapter Three | Disappointments and Setbacks 47

Chapter Four | Vision Casting and Culture Building 61

Chapter Five | If God Wants me to be Successful,
Why is it so Hard? 75

Chapter Six | Created with Purpose 89

Chapter Seven | Expectations, Accountability and Correction 97

Chapter Eight | Discovering Your Leadership Style 115

Chapter Nine | Decisions, Decisions, Decisions 125

Chapter Ten | Craving Greatness 143

Chapter Eleven | Control Versus Influence 153

Chapter Twelve | Work Life Balance: Is That a Real Thing? 165

Chapter Thirteen | God's Protection 183

Chapter Fourteen | The Wrap Up 197

Author's Notes 203

Sources 205

Acknowledgments

I've heard other authors talk about birthing a book, and I never really understood it until I put all the words within the pages of this book. It has been a labor of love, a sacrifice, a period of being stretched. God has supernaturally given me time to write when there didn't seem to be time. Most of the words found within were written during a horrific time in our lives. I now know it was meant to be that way so I can give God all the glory for the contents.

I'm so thankful for my husband, David, who has supported me and my writing from the very beginning. He has always believed in me, telling me I have something to offer the world and that I needed to put myself out there. He has been my biggest source of encouragement during this entire journey. He is actually the one who said, "Maybe God wants you to write about our business." On nights I felt anointed to write, he made sure our boys were taken care of and gave me the space I needed.

Thank you to my boys, Isaiah and Spencer, for always encouraging me, as well. Isaiah would say, "Momma, I haven't seen you writing anything in awhile," and it motivated me to keep going. I realized he was watching me to see if I would finish what I had started. When about to bang my head against the computer screen out of frustration, Spencer would walk up and say, "I love you, Momma." I regained my mental capacities, felt love and edification from his tiny but mighty soul, and continued writing.

I'm thankful for Sara Moseley and Kay Wammack who weren't afraid of editing my book with truth but with love in their hearts. They are two very talented grammar queens. A big thank you to Dede Simmons for her awesome cover design and formatting skills. She's a master creator, and I'm honored she would choose to help me with this project. Also, I have to thank Emily Garcia for the amazing watercolor painting found on the front cover. I asked her to pray about what the cover should look like, and we both trusted the Holy Spirit to reveal it to her. It's perfect!

I also have to thank my staff for their endless support of asking me when the book would be ready and for providing me with awesome stories while stretching me to fulfill God's call upon my life.

Foreword

I was around the age of seven when I wrote my first "book." It was hardly a book but more a story I crafted regarding a family of cats and their journey to and from church on a Sunday. I remember drawing and coloring pictures on each page of the loose- leaf, wide-ruled, notebook paper. I tied it together with shoe string bows made from red yarn. I felt so proud of my accomplishment, and I think I still have that little creation tucked away in a tote somewhere in my attic. I was a child hoarder.

Fast forward to the present day. I have never stopped writing. Usually, it's journaling, or social media posting, or blogging. But the desire in my heart to publish a book has always burned deep. And not just any book, but a book with purpose and meaning serving as a source of help for those who read it. It feels like there is something planted into my being beckoning me to write. When I was younger, my motives probably weren't right. But God has done a work in me. There's been a refining of my heart, a purifying. At times, I tried to shake writing all together. I asked God to take the desire away from me if it was not what He wanted, but the desire has never left. After high school, I attended college, got married, had a couple of boys, and have worked full-time for most of my adult life. Finding the time to write a book overwhelmed me. I remember the night my husband told me I needed to start writing. I wasn't sure what my topic would be at that time. I always imagined it being something moms or wives could relate to, but that's not what my story morphed into at all. God had taken my dream of writing a book and my husband's dream of business ownership and intertwined them together. My book began to take form around the concept of living for Jesus while running a business. I had a difficult time finding any information on this topic when I started working with my husband in business.

I feel a calling to the ministry. I want to take Jesus with me everywhere I go. I want to lead with him and be led by him as I allow his Holy Spirit to empower me. I have found most of my ministry takes place outside the walls of a church. Maybe you are feeling this same calling from the Lord to be in ministry, but it doesn't seem like the church doors are opening for you. You can do ministry right where you are making an impact on your community and ultimately your world. Throughout the book, I will refer to staff, employees, and team members, but feel free to replace those words with words that represent the people in your life you are leading or want to lead. I needed this years ago when I was desperate to plug in to ministry, but I had a hard time figuring out exactly how to do so as I searched online job postings for "church jobs." I needed the book again on my first day as a leader of a small business. And I still benefit from the words within the pages when I need reminding of God's goodness and His promises to me.

After writing most of the content, I read it for the first time, making multiple edits and changes, fretting over every chapter. At one point, I thought about giving up and just keeping the stories inside of it to myself. I said to God, "Lord, I don't have anything to offer anyone. I think I should just give up on this." The Holy Spirit spoke to me in the way only He can, "Your book is full of scriptures, my Holy word, and even though your words may return void, my words never do." It was at that moment I sighed and breathed a little deeper. I realized it wasn't up to me. It's all up to Him, and it always has been. It's only my job to cast the seeds and pray they reach fertile ground so God can reap a harvest and be glorified within the pages of our humble hustle to not only be like Jesus in the workplace but to lead alongside him on our journey to advance the kingdom of God outside the walls of a church.

Chapter One

FINDING THE WHY

"I want to quit!" It's a statement I grumble in my mind over and over during the past few years of owning a small business with my husband, David. Immediately after I entertain the thought, guilt follows. How could I even think about giving up on the place I believe God has sent me? I shrug off the guilt and give myself a pep talk. "You put a lot of prayer into this decision, and you know God led you to this place — even when you don't want to be here."

I cry myself to sleep at night as I long for a season in life where I can catch my breath before another sucker punch to my stomach causing a paralyzing anxiety. I've told David several times, "Maybe I just need to medicate myself. Wouldn't that make things easier?" It seems there's a pill for most things, but I know a quick fix pill isn't the answer to the distress I feel.

I certainly considered medication the morning I received one of our biggest business blows. I wasn't prepared for the news. The area in which our business is located had experienced heavy rain for days, and our thirty thousand square foot warehouse, holding our livelihood, had been submerged in two feet of water. Suddenly, we were considered flood victims by the local news and everyone in our community. Emotions of sadness, anger, defeat, but also perseverance rose up inside of me simultaneously. How would we ever survive such a catastrophe?

I had wrestled with the idea of quitting in the past, but now I had to truly count the cost. In the past, I had thought about searching for a job where I could clock-in and out, leaving the stress of leadership behind. In fact, I have had several of those jobs. My work stress level was lower. I worked hard, gave my best, and went home. In the wake of the flood, it sounded even more appealing. Leadership. Why did I want it in the first place? It's so romanticized and glamorized in our culture, but most of the time it's anything but. I wondered if I would be happier following someone else's lead than being in this uncomfortable and often isolating position. And as I waded around in the flood waters, I could no longer play theoretical games. We were being watched by our community, employees, and family on how we were going to walk our faith out. We had to know if we were going to continue, and we had to have a compelling reason to do so. We had no idea what the future held for us, our employees, or our business. All we knew was we trusted God to wade through it all with us. It's in these moments of introspection that I must remind myself of the WHY.

My WHY, and David's WHY is simply stated as workplace ministry. We will delve into what that actually means in the chapters to follow. With so much loss surrounding us, we had to walk out a difficult journey in the days and months to come. Some days were unimaginably hard. We'll get to the end of the story soon enough. For now, let's take a look at the beginning.

THE BACK STORY

I'd love to take you on the journey with me, but first, you may need a bit of background information on what kind of business we have and how it started.

FINDING THE WHY   1

My in-laws, Ricky and Kathy, started a wholesale floral company over 40 years ago. The business was created during the era of lava lamps, Charlie's Angels, and bell bottom jeans. They sold pre-made floral arrangements and supplies to retailers near and far. David grew up in the industry – it's really all he has ever known. When he was supposed to begin college, he found himself behind the wheel of a sales truck making rounds on his Dad's route. He felt he needed to take on more responsibility in his family's business. He also had no clue what he wanted to do with his life or what major to choose. He once flustered his college career counselor by telling her that what he really wanted to be was a professional fisherman. At least he was honest.

After working in the business in a full-time capacity, it didn't take long for his artistic abilities and creativity to be noticed. Soon, he was asked by other companies to design and develop products, and the items he designed sold well. The manufacturing companies love to see him coming, because they know he is able to make quality products with affordable prices. He designs seasonal and floral decor products using a variety of mediums such as: metal, acrylic, styrofoam, and wood. Before long, he had his own product line, the namesake of our business, David Christopher's Collection. Creativity is his passion, and he has found his place in a world of endless career possibilities. More importantly, he has never looked back with regret. Well, with the exception of wanting to be a professional fisherman, but he'll live.

When I met David, I was a graduate student pursuing a counseling degree while working at a local university as an academic advisor. Shortly afterward, I achieved my dream of working as a career counselor. I loved helping college students prepare for the future by guiding them through the decision-making process, helping them assemble resumes and preparing for job interviews. I taught courses and presented useful information to students in a variety

1 LEADING WITH JESUS

of classes. After a couple of years, I was promoted to an assistant director role. I was able to do what I loved and assisted in leading more than a few people. It was a dream job and I loved it. I couldn't imagine doing anything else for the next twenty or so years.

During this same time, David's wholesale floral business had morphed into an import company, as well as a retail store. The stress from managing multiple businesses was monumental for him. I saw fatigue in his eyes day-in and day-out, and I often encouraged him to think hard about whether or not the business was something he wanted to continue or if he had another dream job in mind. After all, career counseling wasn't just for my students at the local university. His reply was always, "This is where God wants me" referring to the family business, David Christopher's.

Wow! At the time, I didn't know if I believed him. I thought, if God wants you there, why in the world is it so hard? Whenever he came home talking about financial struggles or personnel issues I would find myself thinking and even once told him outright, "That doesn't sound like what God wants for you."

I was wrong. There, I said it. I'll share more about the depth of how wrong I was later, but for now, I'll say it again: I. WAS. WRONG. As I watched David patiently remain faithful to where God had called him, through good times and bad, I began to realize God is more interested in developing our character than delivering us from our circumstances. Managing a business comes with lots of character building — heaps and heaps.

My husband would sometimes joke with me about joining the family business, and I always laughed and said, "You're crazy! Why in the world would I leave a job I love to come to work with you and all the chaotic issues you encounter daily?" I told him I needed to know I was making a difference by helping people. Besides, I had awesome perks like great health insurance and lots of vacation time. While I appreciate artistic endeavors, I didn't see the value in what he was doing when applied to humanity. It just seemed like creating products and making sales to me. Plus, I didn't want to look that stressed out when I got home from work in the afternoons.

I was comfortable in my work bubble and with my life until I began to have chronic jaw problems. Eventually my jaw issues led me to the surgery table where damaged discs that I didn't even know existed had to be repaired. People who know me would probably tell you it's because I talk too much, and they are probably right. It was during the intense moments of pain following surgery that I began to question whether or not I would be able to continue working at the university. I had to do so much talking, and the pain had become unbearable. I began to pray and ask God for direction for my life. At the same time, David needed someone to take care of social media, marketing, and human resources for his growing businesses. He told me, "You don't have to come to work with me, but if you don't, I will need to hire someone to do these jobs. I'm really hoping it's you, though."

PRAYER AND FASTING

We prayed and fasted for several weeks. Fasting is a biblical practice of denying yourself food or some other earthly desire in order to retrain your hunger to seek after God instead. In essence, it helps you align your mind, will and spirit with God's mind, will and Spirit. To put it in modern terms, fasting is like going out to dinner with Jesus, and putting your phone away, so you can focus on Him. At first, denying yourself the pleasure of checking your phone will feel difficult, but by denying the desire you are better able to connect with Him, listen and enjoy His presence. We knew it was going to take prayer and fasting to experience the breakthrough we needed.

As we denied our flesh, we dug into God's word and prayed desperately to hear God's will. He was faithful to reveal to us my next move: I had to join the family business. That's right, I HAD to join. I

1 LEADING WITH JESUS

didn't want to join. I cried. I asked, "Why?" I wasn't excited or thrilled to be making this move, but I knew it was where the Lord wanted me. I had a heart for ministry and helping people and I didn't see how I was going to be able to do either of those things with this career change. I felt like I was sacrificing my dream for David's. I know God never misguides us, and He always leads us to higher ground. I understand He is always making a way, and He sees the big picture when I don't. But, I am still a human with emotions, and I felt angry.

Three years later, I am on the other side of my initial anger, but if I'm being honest, I still feel angry when things aren't going well. It burns deep and wide. My soul groans with frustration. Just because I'm a Christian doesn't mean I'm immune to this emotion. I feel the anger when coworkers take advantage of me or of other team members. I feel it when I know I am being lied to, or when a customer is creating a situation, and I have to bend and flex to keep things proper even though in real life the customer is not always right. I feel it when I am tired, exhausted and run down. I am a daughter of the King, a wife, a mom, and a business owner—in that order, but sometimes the order gets swapped around, and business owner takes precedence over everything else, and I get angry. Then, I cry. The bitter taste of tears reminds me of my circumstances until I remind myself of Psalm 56:8, *"You keep track of all my sorrows. You have collected all my tears in your bottle. You have recorded each one in your book."* The salty taste of my tears also reminds me God has called me to be salt and light. (Matthew 5:13-16)

All at once I am humbled and grateful. I have a God who collects each tear. No matter what the cause of my pain is that day, He cares for me. He takes me in His arms and holds me. He collected a lot of tears on the day of the flood. In these moments, I am reminded of how much closer I draw to the Father when I am hurting. During the pain and long-suffering, I call upon His name and He rescues me. Again and again, He rescues me and reminds me why He has called me to do what I am doing. He reminds me I am not alone. The rescuing can seem to take forever. During moments of my deepest despair, I wonder if it's coming at all. I wonder if He is coming to my aid or if maybe I have fallen out of His favor.

It's so easy to grow weary, even when you know your WHY. Galatians 6:9 tell us, *"Let us not become weary of doing good for at the proper time, we will reap the harvest."* Oftentimes, it feels like we are just sowing seeds and never seeing the fruits of our labor or experiencing a harvest, but God promised us we will, and He is faithful to ALL of His promises. Our purpose can be to sow the seeds or reap the harvest. Sometimes, we get to do both, but it can be rare. We can't give up on our WHY when we aren't seeing the results we think we should be seeing.

LACE UP YOUR ROLLER SKATES

Since I'm a mom, part of my WHY relates to my two boys, Isaiah, my oldest, and Spencer, my youngest. A few months ago I went roller skating with my youngest son at an after school function. Spencer wanted to learn how to roller skate, but was hesitant to try, because the last time it didn't go so well. His precious attempts had fallen flat. No pun intended. He's hesitant about a lot of things these days. He lives reserved and afraid of failure. I can relate to the fear of failure.

Agreeing to participate with him, I laced up the old rental skates — stinky from someone else's feet, and took a few spins around the rink as he watched from the sidelines. I touched my toe stop to the floor as I got closer to his spot on the carpeted bench. He had been intently watching me, taking in my every stride.

"You ready to try?" I asked, extending my hand towards him.

"How did you get so good?" He asked.

I laughed, "Practice. Lots of practice."

"I knew you would say that," he replied.

1 LEADING WITH JESUS

I didn't want to ask him to do anything I wasn't willing to do myself, so I took his hand, explaining each motion. He watched my feet and attempted to copy my movements. I was teaching by doing. He was learning by observing. It reminded me of how Jesus teaches us. He has experienced every frustration, temptation and human emotion we experience, and throughout the Bible, He shows us how to handle each difficulty.

"You have to keep moving your feet to go forward," I instructed my son. I knew if he stopped, he would fall or possibly get knocked down by another skater. Roller skating is a balancing act, and I was his sidekick, helping him stay upright. After circling the floor a couple of times with me, our hands clasped tightly, disco lights flashing an array of colors, music moving our bodies, he began skating solo. Even though I taught him the basics, he found his own groove. His stride was understandably shorter, slower and a little less balanced, but he was skating all the same.

Choosing to be like Jesus in the marketplace is a balancing act, too. However, if you include Him in your plans and invite Him to go with you, eventually you find your groove.

I took a break and sat on the side watching Spencer make his rounds. He only made eye contact with me for a brief moment so as not to lose his balance. I thought of all the nights I skated as a child. I absolutely loved it then, and I still do, today. At the end of the night, we went home with sore feet and legs from our efforts. We had used muscles we hadn't used in some time. It was to be expected.

Leading like Jesus comes with aches and pains, too. Showing people how to do something is more effective than telling them. Jesus led by His example, so it's not enough for us to tell people how to live like Jesus. We have to show them. We cannot ask others to do what we're not willing to do. Sometimes people need us to hold their hands and help them keep their balance for a few rounds. Sometimes people don't do things exactly like we would do them, but it doesn't mean their ways are wrong and our ways are right. Their ways may be different, but we both make it around the rink. People need to find their own groove and their own path.

Although people and paths are different, truth is uncompromising. Once you stop following the greatest Teacher in moving in the right direction, you will fall or get knocked down. Sitting on the sidelines is no place to be either. If you never put on skates, you'll never learn. Sure, it may not always look pretty, and there will be times it's downright uncomfortable, but getting out there and putting in the work is critical to your success, and it will take work.

What is your WHY? Why do you do what you do day in and day out? If you aren't sure, you will find plenty of excuses to quit. Your days in leadership will be even harder than you can imagine as you don't have a reason to continue pressing forward towards God's plan for you and your life. When rejection comes, and it will, it will take your why to propel you forward; to keep you moving forward; to keep you engaged with the goal.

When we get tired of the work and want to quit, we begin to ask questions like, "What's the point?" When we hit the floor, flesh burning and torn, we have to get back up, dust ourselves and keep going. We must keep showing up, keep worshiping, keep praying, keep studying God's word and keep asking Him for wisdom.

When I feel anger and the pain, I remember my WHY. I recall that God has strategically placed me in my position, and He wants me here for a reason. He has a WHY, too:

> He wants me to make an impact for Jesus in the lives of the individuals I have the honor to mentor. He wants me to make a difference in the organizations we support through service or with financial contributions. He wants me to pray for those who call our store, "their happy place." And He wants me to focus on the potential to do even more good as our business succeeds.

1 LEADING WITH JESUS

REMEMBERING YOUR WHY

When the money is low and the bills are mounting, I remind myself that my WHY is not financial gain; it is making a difference in the lives of everyone I encounter and allowing God to make a difference in me. Being Jesus in the workplace, the marketplace, is my WHY. He has a purpose and a destiny for me to fulfill. I am not here by mistake or accident. Guess what? God has a purpose and a destiny for you, as well. You have a purpose only you can fill with God's help. We are called to be His servants not vice versa. To figure out your why, ask yourself a few questions:

- Who all does my leadership impact?
- What kind of difference am I making in the lives of those around me?
- What am I sowing into other than my business?
- What am I trying to accomplish through my leadership and my influence? Is it for my glory or God's?

Our world needs Jesus in a desperate way; therefore, our world needs more leaders who look like Jesus and who lead with him. You can be the kind of leader you would want to follow. If you have been washed by the blood of the lamb, you have something to offer those around you. You have something unique inside of you God can use to bring heaven to earth. But you have to be ready to fight the good fight and stop making "I quit" statements. When the enemy whispers, "What do you have to offer?" You can boldly reply, "JESUS!"

My journey as a leader for Jesus may look a lot like yours or a lot different from yours, but I hope as you read this book you feel understood and encouraged to keep following God's will for your life. When it's all over, and we are called home, we get to trade in our stinky, worn, rental skates for a brand new pair. What are you waiting

FINDING THE WHY 1

for? Lace up, get out there, and be willing to help someone else as you circle the rink of life, remember you why, and never give up. After all, that's what Jesus would do.

EXERCISE

1. Stop and ask God to reveal to you if you are in the middle of His will and plan. God equips us before He sends us, and if He sends us, we can be confident we are equipped to handle whatever comes our way. Our WHY has to be bigger than making money and providing for ourselves. Yes, those things are important and necessary, but God's WHY is bigger than our needs and wants.

2. Do you need a breakthrough in your life? Have you tried prayer and fasting? If not, why not start today.

Make it a priority to know your WHY so quitting isn't an option.

Chapter Two

JESUS IN THE MARKETPLACE: THE BASICS

It took months of me working before I began to really see the difference our business was making in the lives of others. I think back to conversations David and I had before I joined "the crazy." There were times I pleaded, "Wouldn't closing the businesses and working for someone else be better? You could make more money and have less stress." The day our store flooded was no different. I asked again. Each time he would reply, "But what about…" and he would begin to list the names of various employees on our team. He sincerely cared for every person and many times through individual conversations he shared the love of Jesus with them. His love was contagious and I soon found myself loving our team, too. During the days of clean up following the flood, our goal was to stay encouraged and to encourage those around us. Some days it was extremely difficult, but God girded us up in strength and gave us hope through His people who surrounded us each day in the form of volunteers and paid staff.

THE OVERFLOW

Ministry is an overflow of who you are in Christ that bubbles

2 LEADING WITH JESUS

up from inside and pours into the lives of those around you. It's not something you can turn on and off. At least it shouldn't be unless you are taking a rest to refill and refresh— a topic I'll share more about later. If you are disciplined in your determination to seek Jesus first and live for Him, your ministry to others will flow continuously. Faith should be sewn into the very fabric of our being and fuel our hope and resolve as we experience life together.

Marketplace is defined by Merriam-Webster in several different ways:

1. An open square or place in a town where markets or public sales are held
2. The world of trade or economic activity-the everyday world.

Basically, the marketplace is our world. It's where we buy, where we sell, and where we live our lives. It's where we attend school and work. Most of us go into the marketplace each and every day; therefore, we are presented with numerous opportunities, most of which we pass up, to be Jesus to those around us. Your primary marketplace may be where you run your small business or lead your team. It could be where you teach music lessons or sell a service. Or maybe it's when you are checking out at the grocery store, and you notice the person behind you in line looks like she could use a kind word. Deciding to act more like Jesus in our world, our marketplace, takes walking intentionally and seeking out people who need what we have to offer.

Jesus calls all believers the church, meaning the church is a living, breathing body and not just a building we go to on Sundays and for small group meetings. Romans 12: 4-5 tells us, *"For as in one body we have many members, and the members do not all have the same function, so we, though many, are one body in Christ, and individually members one of another."* If you are a Christian, a Christ bearer, you should be the church and claim ground for Jesus wherever you tread.

Even if you are treading in nasty, murky rainwater wearing yesterday's clothes exhausted from long days and excruciating hours of work.

During a prayer and fast at our church, I led a devotional on being a witness for Christ. My prayer focus was specifically on asking God for more opportunities to share Him. I also asked for courage and boldness. Who knew the answer to this prayer would come the same night as I stopped by a local fast food restaurant to pick up sandwiches for our boys?

The person helping us treated us so poorly I was in shock. I tried to make small talk with her, and she refused to speak to me. She prepared our food, rang up our purchase, and then handed me the bag of sandwiches without so much as a thank you. David made it a point to thank her. She stared at us like we were from another galaxy. As we left, I was already formulating my complaint against her. My fingers quickly opened Google on my cell phone in an attempt to find the restaurant review tab and light into her so that someone in management could set her straight and teach her better customer service. After all, I would want someone to tell me if my employees had behaved the way she had.

I selected the location of the restaurant, and as I started typing my comments about our experience, I heard the Holy Spirit ask, "Didn't you ask me for an opportunity? Didn't you ask me for boldness?" I stopped, loosely dropping my phone into my lap. God had my attention. "Yes, Lord." I felt like a fool. God had put us face to face with someone who needed him desperately immediately following a prayer meeting. I had failed miserably at answering His call. I was in disbelief at myself and how not attuned I was to His spirit.

David and I discussed the situation on the way home and decided to pray for her and to ask God for wisdom on our next steps. We sat at our kitchen table as David led a prayer calling out her name to the Lord. When the prayer was finished, we both agreed I should call the restaurant, ask for the young girl, and encourage her.

2 LEADING WITH JESUS

I felt extremely awkward calling, and I am sure I stuttered as I said, "We were just in getting some sandwiches. You seemed to be having a bad night. I have had those kinds of nights, and I know how much it means just to know someone cares. And we want you to know that we care, and we felt compelled to pray for you and your situation. We are believing your situation will improve."

A brief silence was on the other end of the line before I heard, "Thank you. I really appreciate that." I proceeded to tell her to have a good night, and our phone call ended. I felt like I had been obedient to what the Lord wanted me to do. I hated the fact that I missed the first opportunity, but I was thankful for a second chance to get it right.

If you continue reading in Romans 12, verses 6-8 will tell you how you are equipped to do what God has called you to do. *"Having gifts that differ according to the grace given to us, let us use them: if prophecy, in proportion to our faith; if service, in our serving; the one who teaches, in his teaching; the one who exhorts, in his exhortation; the one who contributes, in generosity; the one who leads, with zeal; the one who does acts of mercy, with cheerfulness."*

You have gifts inside of you in which God can use to win the lost, show His love, and advance His kingdom here on earth. He needs us to use these gifts in our workplaces and sandwich shop visits. If everyone decides to only try to advance the kingdom while on a mission trip, at a church event, or when they land a job within the walls of a church, so many opportunities will be missed. When you accepted Jesus, you accepted a calling to share the gospel in all places.

Romans 12 lists marks of a true Christian. How many of these marks do you resemble? Where could you improve?

- Loves genuinely
- Abhors what's evil; holding fast to the good
- Loves one another with brotherly affection
- Outdoes one another in showing honor

JESUS IN THE MARKETPLACE: THE BASICS 2

- Not lazy or slothful but full of zeal
- Fervent in spirit
- Patient during tribulations
- Prays constantly
- Contributes to the needs of the saints and seeking to show hospitality
- Blesses those who persecute you; do not curse them
- Lives in harmony with one another
- Not haughty or prideful
- Never wise in your own sight
- Repays no one's evil with evil; allow God to avenge you

STOPPING TO PRAY

In our marketplace, celebrating wins and stopping to pray when needed are both important to us. We celebrate the joys of our teammates, from adoptions and births, to anniversaries and graduations. We pray for our coworkers and mourn with them during hard seasons — sicknesses, divorces, financial setbacks. In our business, it is commonplace to pull someone aside and pray, and it has made a world of difference. While enduring the days following the flood, we were pulled aside a lot by employees, family, and friends. Prayer changes us. It changes those who pray with us. It helps us to focus our minds on the One who holds all the answers and who deserves all of our praises.

You can and you should incorporate prayer into your leadership role. Granted, you must be careful about whom you lay your hands upon. 2 Timothy 5:22 tells us, *"Do not be hasty in the laying on of hands, nor take part in the sins of others; keep yourself pure."* There can be a transference of spirits when you lay hands on someone or when you allow someone to lay hands on you. If you do feel compelled to lay hands on someone when you pray, ask for

2 LEADING WITH JESUS

permission. Never assume it's okay. Be bold and mention prayer to those around you. For example, while taking a coworker out to lunch, ask if she minds if you pray to bless the food. You can even ask your server if he or she has any prayer needs. I always like to listen to the Holy Spirit before asking the last question. Most of the time, people are receptive to prayer, but not always. Praying before or at the conclusion of a staff meeting is also a good practice to introduce those around you to prayer. Before I was in a leadership role, I used to pray with my coworkers. It amazed me that some had never been prayed over by anyone. Taking the initiative to pray for someone is leading them to Christ. It's inviting the person into His presence along with you. And if you are ever not sure how to pray, remember Jesus's example in Matthew 6: 11-14:

> *"Our Father in heaven,*
> *Hallowed be your name.*
> *Your kingdom come,*
> *your will be done,*
> *on earth as it is in heaven.*
> *Give us this day our daily bread,*
> *and forgive us our debts,*
> *As we also have forgiven our debtors.*
> *And lead us not into temptation,*
> *but deliver us from evil."*

The King James version ends verse 15 with, *"For thine is the kingdom, and the power, and the glory for ever. Amen."*

If I am ever unsure what to pray, this is my go-to prayer. If you haven't committed it to heart, I suggest you take time to do so. Memorize it, understand it, and make a note of the things covered in the prayer. Jesus begins this prayer by honoring God and making reference to his hallowed name. He comes into agreement with the

Lord for His will to be done on earth, because he knows God's will is much better than his own. He asks for heaven to come to earth, for daily needs to be met, and he asks for forgiveness and confesses he has forgiven those who have sinned against him. He asks God to keep him away from temptation and out of the powerful hands of Satan.

    Within this book of Matthew, Jesus also tells the people to go into their prayer closets and pray in secret. Can you remember the last time you applied that principle to your life and to your role as a leader? It reminds me of the movie, "The War Room" where the main character had a closet she had reserved for prayer. It was her meeting place with God. What a wonderful concept to prepare a place to take it all to the Lord. It seems like I am usually in bed, in the middle of the night, when prayer comes the easiest to me. It's quiet, dark, and everyone is asleep. Distractions are a minimum. I begin by thanking God and telling Him I love Him. It's a great place for you to begin, as well. The next time you can't sleep at night, ask God, "Is there something you want to say to me?" And remain quiet until you hear from Him.

    I will be the first to admit answered prayers don't always come as soon as I would like. I can get very impatient as I wait on God to orchestrate His plan, but it doesn't stop me from petitioning Him on a daily basis.

    I remember walking to a team member's office to discuss a few things with him, but as I approached the door, I could hear him softly saying, "Well, let me pray with you about that. Would it be okay?" As I got closer, I heard him begin the prayer, so I walked away smiling, full of gratitude he had taken the opportunity to share love with one of our customers. Despite the numerous tasks on his plate, he had not forgotten he was dealing with a person with flesh and bones, who needed a listening ear. He was praying for the customer out of his overflow. Opportunities for marketplace ministry often happen while

2 LEADING WITH JESUS

we are busy getting things done, landing softly on our work plates somewhere between spreadsheets and phone calls.

I have story after story of team members who stopped to pray. One customer, who was battling cancer, stopped in often. She said our store was her happy place. We prayed over her multiple times and were grateful she allowed us to share her burden and love her as she journeyed through a dark season. Several of us cried the day we learned she had finished her honorable battle and gone home to be with Jesus. When we saw her beautiful face in the obituary of a local news source, we grieved her smile and sweet spirit. But we rejoiced knowing she was with her Lord and Savior. We had gotten to know her as a customer, but when she departed this world, she was our friend. Relationships are key to running any successful business, but our connections have to be genuine in order to make a lasting impression. Connections can begin with prayer.

THE STORY OF LYDIA

You don't have to report to work at a church building every day to be in ministry. In fact, Jesus didn't. Sure, many people are called to work at and for the church in an official capacity. Goodness, what would we do without those folks? But if we think we have to have a specific title to do ministry, then ministry is nothing more than a label to us and not an outpouring of Christ through us.

In the book of 2 Corinthians, Paul writes about a lady called Lydia. Some believe Lydia to be her real name while others believe Lydia to mean "The Lydian," because her home was in Thyatira, a city of Lydia, a Macedonia colony. *"And on the Sabbath day we went outside the gate to the riverside, where we supposed there was a place of prayers, and we sat down and spoke to the women who had come together. One who heard us was a woman named Lydia, from the city of Thyatira, a seller of purple goods, who was a worshipper of God.*

The Lord opened her heart to pay attention to what was said by Paul. And after she was baptized, and her household as well, she urged us, saying, 'If you have judged me to be faithful to the Lord, come to my house and stay.' And she prevailed upon us." (Acts 16:13-15).

Scripture doesn't tell us much about Lydia, but we know she worshipped God and then she accepted Christ and was baptized. It also seems she shared Jesus with her household, because they, too, were baptized. And we know she was a business woman since the word mentions her to be a "seller of purple." Perhaps she was in the business of hand dying fabric. Since she had a home with servants, and she invited Paul and Silas to stay with her, it is thought she did well for herself. I'm sure Lydia had a lot of work to do during her daily grind, but she had an open heart to what Paul was teaching. Her focus was not only on her competitive edge of how many pieces she could finish in a day; she was wise to recognize the importance of prayer and worship. She was literally baptized in her marketplace for all of those around her to see. In the same river in which she dyed fabric purple, she was washed white as snow. It was a public and brave declaration of her faith in Christ since she was surrounded by many Jewish people. Imagine the emotions she may have felt thinking about whether or not she would upset her family, her customers, or her community with her decision to so openly follow Jesus. Or what whispers may have been said as she walked Paul and Silas, after being released from prison, bruised and beaten, to her home. I believe she continued onward in her business, knowing her why, after she was baptized. She had tasted truth and the royal robe of salvation had been placed upon her shoulders by her Creator. She knew there was nothing more important than carrying the love of Christ to her family and to her marketplace. Her example to us, as leaders, is a pertinent one as we seek to put our faith in action.

2 LEADING WITH JESUS

REPRESENTING JESUS WELL

As bearers of Christ's name and carriers of his light and love, we have the awesome privilege of representing Jesus wherever we go. The workplace is an awesome location to show the world His love and compassion for people. We don't have to shove the gospel down people's throats for them to catch on. Being like Jesus is a gentle leading. It's making good choices in the presence of others (and when no one is watching). It's patiently attending to a customer who is being crass and rude. It's a customer seeing how you handle an employee who has made a mistake. Demonstrating the patience, grace and kindness of Jesus is working through things in an admirable way without yelling, condemning or shaming. It's a delicate dance between being taken advantage of and requiring accountability. We must keep Jesus on the forefront of our thoughts and actions. Yes, there will be times we miss the mark, but if we are faithful to get back on track and return to our role of being a light in the darkness, we will experience the power and joy of ministry in action.

It's easy to talk about faith, quote scriptures and wear t-shirts with cute wording about needing Jesus and coffee. However, walking out what we believe and know to be true can be grueling and painful. When we choose to live like Jesus in our marketplace, and not just at church on Sunday or in a small group meeting, we travel a straight and narrow road, and there's nothing cute about it.

A lot of people don't know who Jesus is, and they are looking to us to show them. Even people who claim to be believers don't fully know or understand all of His characteristics. His teachings are simple enough to be understood by a child, and yet there are infinite multi-faceted layers of complexity and mystery.

One day at work, I was explaining to someone how Jesus was not a pushover, and she seemed surprised. It was in the moment that I was able to explain how we, as believers, don't have to be pushovers either. Jesus was more effectively able to correct those who knew He loved them. His acts of love proved to people He wasn't at all about a selfish lifestyle. Our customers and fellow coworkers must know we care about them first and foremost if leading with Jesus is our goal. Even if marketplace ministry is not our primary goal, it should be our intention, as a Christian, to show honor, love and respect to all we encounter.

People are drawn to Jesus when they hear of His personal, unconditional love for them. He is prayerful, wise, virtuous, humble, obedient, patient, charitable, giving and forgiving. And we are made in His image. Each day, as we strive to be more and more like Him, we lead those around us to be more like Him, as well. It's good to tell the people under your care that you are sorry when you make a mistake. It's good for them to see you are human and that you are trying your best to lead them, but you don't have it all figured out. When we were faced with the torrential downpours of rain, we told our employees we didn't know what the future looked like, but we trusted God to get us through it all. They respected us admitting we didn't have it all figured out.

APOLOGIZE OFTEN

As a parent and as an employer, I have had to apologize. It's not the most fun to have to admit, "Hey, I am the one in charge here, but I messed up." One particular incident stands out to me. I had a discussion with a new hire about one of our rules. I felt like the new hire might be in violation of the policy, so I was on high alert. Another of my loyal employees asked me a question leading me to think maybe he was in violation of this same policy; although my gut told me he was not. I felt it my duty to ask. My questioning of him hurt. In retrospect, questioning him was not my brightest idea. However, I was able to say, "I'm sorry," and thankfully, he forgave me.

2 LEADING WITH JESUS

Another instance which comes to mind involves David. In the wake of the flood, a year later, David opened up a staff meeting with vulnerable words letting our employees know he had not been the leader he wanted to be. He admitted to being too tired and too slow to praise but too quick to criticize. He had been leading out of a place of exhaustion and bad circumstances, but he vowed to encourage more, to be more organized, and to ramp up his follow-through game. It was evident our team had opened their hearts to his confessions. Maybe there's an apology you need to make today to someone on your team to heal hearts and bind up wounds.

It's not easy admitting shortcomings to those we lead, but it's imperative to a healthy team. Reflect on the last time you admitted fault to a team member. If it's been awhile, spend some time thinking about times you could have seized an opportunity to hold yourself accountable to the same standards you have set for your team. It's amazing how we allow ourselves to grow and change, but sometimes we don't extend this same grace to those on our team.

HONESTY, TRANSPARENCY AND TRUST

Honesty, transparency, and trust are critical to building healthy relationships. I remember not long after I joined the company, there was some contention on our team regarding how bonuses would be distributed that year. It was going to be less than most people were expecting, and folks were wondering what they had done wrong to warrant this change in their pay. I am the type of person who wants to get things out in the air so understanding can begin to take form, so I called a meeting.

We described to everyone the amount of debt we were trying to pay off due to the recession, which had happened in 2007, and we shared our plan with them. Once we explained where we were going and our plan to get there, most employees were on board. One even said, "I would rather take less now and keep my job, than to get a bigger bonus, which could cause our company more problems in the long run." He saw the big picture after we were open and honest with him and others about the struggles we were facing. Most people who truly care about their job, coworkers, and company are capable of seeing the big picture when you share the vision with them.

When our business flooded, we had to temporarily relocate. Hold on to your seats, I promise I will tell you the full story in a bit. It was exceedingly hard to pick up and move. The temporary building had less storage and processes that had worked in the previous location were not working in our new location. We basically had one week to move as much salvageable merchandise as possible. A mild case of chaos ensued as we desperately tried to hang on to the reins.

Although we were somewhat seasoned leaders, we were having to learn many things by trial and error. We shared this truth with everyone on the team, letting them know, "We don't know exactly how this is going to work, but we promise to work until we figure it out. In the meantime, know that we value your work efforts and input greatly."

I'm not suggesting you tell employees every intimate detail about your business, but when morale is affected or team members are unhappy because of something they don't understand, it may be time for a "come to Jesus meeting." In all the stories in the Bible about Jesus, He never seems to beat around the bush. Sure, he sometimes taught in parables, but he also boldly said things like, *"Why are you afraid, O you of little faith?"* (Matthew 8:26).

Jesus gives us the amazing story of the laborers in the vineyard in Matthew 20. *"For the kingdom of heaven is like a master of a house who went out early in the morning to hire laborers for his vineyard. After agreeing with the laborers for a denarius a day, he sent them into his vineyard. And going out about the third hour he saw others standing idle in the marketplace, and to them he said, 'You go into the vineyard too, and whatever is right I will give you.' So they went.*

2 LEADING WITH JESUS

Going out again about the sixth hour and the ninth hour, he did the same. And about the eleventh hour he went out and found others standing. And he said to them, 'Why do you stand here idle all day?' They said to him, 'Because no one has hired us.' He said to them, 'You go into the vineyard too.' And when evening came, the owner of the vineyard said to his foreman, 'Call the laborers and pay them their wages, beginning with the last, up to the first.' And when those hired about the eleventh hour came, each of them received a denarius. Now when those hired first came, they thought they would receive more, but each of them also received a denarius. And on receiving it they grumbled at the master of the house, saying, 'These last worked only one hour, and you have made them equal to us who have borne the burden of the day and the scorching heat.' But he replied to one of them, 'Friend, I am doing you no wrong. Did you not agree with me for a denarius? Take what belongs to you and go. I choose to give to this last worker as I give to you. Am I not allowed to do what I choose with what belongs to me? Or do you begrudge my generosity?' So the last will be first, and the first last."

Jesus is using this parable to speak of the kingdom of heaven and how we can all have the same prize no matter when we accept the call to follow Jesus. But I also like how he makes the point that an employer has a right to make decisions regarding how he pays his employees. The employee has the right to refuse or accept the terms. This principle is one in which you should remind yourself of often if people don't agree with your decisions or question how you do what you do. Questions can sometimes lead to better processes and relationships, but sometimes, they lead to wasted time and energy.

The relationship between leaders and team members must be founded on trust. If you have members on your team who you do not trust, or vice versa, you are headed for troubled water. Make it a priority to sit down with people and discuss trust with them in a raw and real way. Reiterate you care about them and their well-being, reminding them you are making the best decisions you can on behalf of them and the business.

Trust is also a requirement for a healthy relationship with God. We must trust Him with our lives and business. We must believe Him when He says He will never leave us nor forsake us (Hebrews 13:5). We must empathize when our team members, at times, when they don't fully trust us—because if we are honest, there are times we don't fully trust God. Unfortunately, many times I have trusted in myself and been stubborn in trying to do things on my own. It's an easy trap to fall into. Fortunately, God is faithful to rescue me from myself, as He is to all people — when we humble ourselves and cry out to Him. It's important to be able to put our pride aside and ask for help when we need it.

I have had the trust conversation with many of my team members. Each time I do, I am reminded to trust God. I can almost hear Him telling me what I am telling my team, "If we don't trust one another, this work relationship is going to be miserable and we will never fulfill our goals and potential, much less reach our destination. You have to believe we love you and want what is best for you. You have to know we are seeking God in our decisions, and we have a lot to lose if we make the wrong decisions."

When I had my first child, Isaiah, I remember realizing God's love for me more than I ever had before. Being a mother gave me a fresh perspective of God's role as our Father and His awesome and enduring love for us. Throughout the process of cleaning up and rebuilding after the flood, I had to remind myself daily of the love God had for me quoting scriptures to keep myself encouraged.

When Spencer, my youngest son, began to have night terrors, I started lying down with him at night so he could go to sleep. I noticed his body physically began to relax as our arms touched. As soon as I would start to leave his bed, the calm left and fear reared its ugly head causing him to breath rapidly and ask, "Will I be okay?" It broke

2 LEADING WITH JESUS

my heart to see him in such distress. I assured him he would be okay, but I could see he still wasn't 100 percent convinced. I took time to explain to him the seasons in life we go through, and although he was in a really bad season, soon he would enter a new season. I promised him he wouldn't always have sleepless nights. I couldn't promise him he would never have another night of unrest, as it would have been a lie, but I assured him he would begin to sleep again. Then, I explained God's love to him, "Do you know Jesus would have died just for you if you were the only human being on the planet?" I lay with him a little longer, praying over him, and listening to worship music. As he drifted off to sleep, I pictured God beside me during the times I'm stressed or worried asking, "Will I be okay, God?" I asked him multiple times a day while throwing away thousands of dollars of wet and damaged merchandise. I asked him when adrenaline rushed through my chest and neck when we found out the insurance money wasn't going to be enough to dig us out of the pit in which the flood had washed us inside of. I pictured how God must feel when I don't fully trust Him and His plan. Just like my son, I want to trust during difficult seasons, but it's a struggle. My heart knows I will be okay, because it is full of the word of God; however, the logical side of my brain questions and runs through a list of things which could potentially go wrong. My fight or flight response can be easily triggered based on past experiences.

My son felt safe with me because I have the position of "momma" in his life. Whether he should trust me or not, he does, because of my position in his life. He feels safe with me. As believers, we have a Father in our lives, who is worth trusting more than any earthly parent. He has proven Himself worthy of our trust over and over again. And as God grabs me by the hand and pulls me out of the various pits in life, my trust for Him grows stronger and stronger. We can confidently have an attitude of knowing God will prepare us for what we have to face in life. We may not feel strong today, as we think of the possibilities of what could go wrong, but we can have full assurance,

JESUS IN THE MARKETPLACE: THE BASICS 2

He will give us the strength we need when the day comes in which we need it.

As I kissed my son's forehead, I wanted him to believe me when I told him he could trust God with all of his heart. As I did, I felt God reminding me that He wanted me to trust Him with all of my heart, too. He wanted me to picture Him right next to me, kissing me on the forehead, saying, "Go to sleep, my child. I've got this." How can we rest and trust in this kind of confidence? By following God's word and intentionally seeking Him moment by moment.

THE UGLY SIDE OF LEADING

David once opened our staff meeting with the verse, *"Seek God's will in all you do, and He will show you the path to take."* (Proverbs 3:6). He explained, as business owners, we are always seeking God for wisdom. The decisions we make are an attempt to make our business better for our employees and our customers. The decisions are never meant to make life hard for anyone. Much thought, prayer and meaning are behind each decision, and sometimes a few tears. We're the first to admit when a decision needs to be changed if we recognize it is not working well. It's not fun to fail, but it's necessary in learning what works and what doesn't.

Having misconceptions about business ownership can't be helped if you've never owned one. Likewise, misconceptions about leadership can't be helped, either, if you have never been in a leadership role. On the outside, leadership takes on the appearance of flexibility and ease. It is living a good life. I think a lot of individuals believe all business owners or people in management roles are swimming in money and have bottomless bank accounts. Some may even believe you, as a leader, have less stress than someone not in an authoritative role.

Truthfully, leadership is rarely glamorous, and it is always hard work filled with grit, guts, and unpredictability. David and I have spent untold hours unclogging toilets; setting up buckets to catch ceiling leaks; praying for customers and employees; catching up on late bills; striving for a work life balance; making decisions that impact everyone; feeling so sick we could vomit over unpleasant workplace issues that have to be addressed; working extremely hard on projects that did not yield the expected fruit; staying up late discussing the "What now?" the "How do we handle this?" and the "Is it worth it?"; shedding tears; questioning ourselves; and asking God to show us His will and His path. We remind ourselves to trust and ask God for more faith. We press on in hope and believe that a difference is being made in the lives of the people we encounter. We strive to emulate Jesus in the marketplace, while simultaneously wondering if we are getting it right.

The stress of work is sometimes more than we can bear on our own, especially when coupled with everyday life, i.e. the HVAC unit goes out; a storm damages the roof; financial expenses crop up unexpectedly; preteen kids start acting like teenagers; impending school changes are announced; my husband's back acts up; etc. I'm sure you could fill in the list I just rattled off with your own challenges. Life is complicated, isn't it? It can't always be packaged up nicely and tied with a big, beautiful bow of hope and joy, can it? One thing is for sure, it is full of despair and moments of weakness.

One day during the flood clean up, I looked around and was shocked at how much work we had accomplished in a short period of time. I knew it was nothing short of the supernatural power of the Holy Spirit working in and through us. We started our days early and ended them late. I worried about whether or not our boys were getting the attention in which they needed, but I didn't know what other choices I had but to continue to help work ourselves out of the mess. I was doubting my abilities and insecurities would give rise to anxiety.

I'm reminded of what the Word says, *"Where I am weak, He is strong"* (2 Corinthians 12:9-11). When we feel like breaking, Jesus holds us together. When we are mentally, emotionally and physically exhausted, He gives us strength. On the days we are gripped with fear about the future He swoops in and reminds us of all of the peace we carry because we are His sons and daughters. He reminds us that His grace is sufficient and He takes care of us every day, without fail. If we didn't have problems, would we talk to Him as much? I'm okay with needing to talk to Him. It's worth the troubled waters we tread. Although, I confess there are times when I feel too consumed, too tired, too unable to concentrate to even offer up a prayer. All I can do is say the Lord's Prayer or tell God, "I trust you, and you know my heart."

God is so compassionate. Not only is He there for us during the times we pray well, with heartfelt fever and focus, but He is there when our only prayer is a half-hearted sigh. Often during hard seasons, I see how God continues to pursue us with His love by planting people in our lives who encourage and cheer us on. They remind us of His word, and like the friends of Moses, who lifted his hands so that Israel might prevail against its enemies (Exodus 17:11-12), our friends reach out their hands and pull up our arms sharing our burden. Somewhere between the day to day grind of sales, marketing, design, human resources, buying, cleaning, and unclogging toilets, God gives us a glimpse of the amazing growth and change He has brought about in those we encounter. We see spiritual growth in each other and in ourselves as we pursue God and His desire for us to lead like Jesus. God offers us abundant grace when we can't seem to hustle enough. All we have to do is ask Him for what we need. He supplies it all.

We must choose to believe God knows what He is doing, even when we don't understand our circumstances. We must trust Him in times of testing when He is developing and refining our character. In every hard decision in which we choose to trust God, what we are really saying yes to is the question He asks all His children, "Can I trust you with a little, so that I may bless you with more?"

The testing of our faith feels like being thrown into a washing machine on a heavy duty, power-wash cycle. While you are being tossed about and feeling like you are spinning out of control, it's difficult to see the good, and very hard to count it all as joy, like the Bible tells us to. But the blessings remain whether we see them or not. In these times, it's important to breath, read the word of God, and actively recall our blessings until we recognize we have more to be thankful for than we realized. One of the primary benefits of trusting God and choosing to look for the good in the midst of difficult circumstances is that it prevents the enemy from stealing our joy.

PRACTICING GRATITUDE

A grateful journal or a journal of answered prayers is a great tool to have in your toolbox. I challenge you to keep a list of all of the things in which you find yourself grateful for and list the times in which God has been faithful to you. On the dark, sad days, when you want to give up, pull out your journal, snuggle into the Lord's goodness and recount your many blessings--name them one by one. This practice will prepare you and propel you forward for another day of commerce ministry.

I don't have it all figured out. I feel fairly inadequate most days, but I am slowly learning to count my blessings instead of my problems. I want to give my attention to what I do have, not to what I don't. One night as I lay in bed, sobbing, I told David, "I'm just so tired." We were experiencing what felt like pure and total hell in all areas of our lives. Although my problems seemed overwhelming at that moment, when I stopped to thank God that I was not battling cancer, nor was I holding the hand of a dying child, I gained what I so desperately needed — perspective. When we obey God in hard times, stopping to thank Him even when we don't feel like it, He always responds. We may not get the immediate deliverance we'd like, but we will always get what we need.

Grateful living is a practice that I have tried and failed at before, but I will keep trying. I will keep thanking God. God is with us as we lead. When we are wondering about the "why, when, and how," He remains the answer. He is our Who that always knows the what, when, where, why and how. He is the Beginning and the End. He is the Victor in our situations, and He calls us overcomers (1 John 5:4).

GUIDED BY HIS SPIRIT

Being Jesus in the marketplace is not always easy, but it is always rewarding. The more you practice, the easier it becomes. Pray with people. Be kind. Share the truth with them every time the opportunity arises. Invite the Holy Spirit in to your workplace every single day. Don't hesitate to march around your building seven times, like Joshua did at Jericho, and declare what you wish to see happen inside the walls in which you find yourself marching around. Have extravagant faith recognizable by those you encounter. In the words of my pastor, Bobby Gourley, "You do the natural. Let God do the supernatural." Read your Bible daily. After all, you can't pour from an empty vessel.

You have to care for yourself by spending time with the Lord in worship and prayer. When you do, you will find you have His strength to do the things you've been called to do. You will feel renewed and refreshed. Ask God to fill you with His Spirit from the tips of your toes to the top of your head, and watch Him overflow into every part of your life—including your business.

2 LEADING WITH JESUS

EXERCISE

1. What are some ways you are already serving as Jesus in the marketplace?

2. What are some new ways you could incorporate Jesus into your daily life?

3. Make it your mission to find someone you can pray with during this upcoming week. Every week afterwards, be on the lookout for who you should pray with, and allow the Holy Spirit to empower you to do so.

4. Instead of attempting to get into the presence of God to talk about what is going wrong or has gone wrong, take the approach of *"entering His gates with thanksgiving, and His courts with praise"* (Psalm 100:4). Start off your prayer by thanking Him for all the good things in your life. Then, praise Him for His ongoing love and faithfulness to you. Practice praying without asking Him for anything but praising Him for all things.

Chapter Three

DISAPPOINTMENTS AND SETBACKS

We got the call at 3:00 a.m. on a Saturday morning. It was one of those mornings we had hoped to sleep in past 7:00 a.m. My husband was planning to go into work later in the day and was expecting an easy morning of bacon, eggs and coffee. We didn't expect to be jolted awake by the vibration of his cell phone. Like most men, he sleeps like a rock. I was groggy as I reached over his shoulder to the side table, "David, it's your dad." Any time a parent calls in the middle of the night, it's an immediate adrenaline rush for me. Over the course of a few years I had gotten the following calls in the middle of the night:

- From my mother, "Your Dad is dying. You need to come now."
- From my father-in-law, "Kathy (my mother-in-law) is in the hospital with complications following surgery."
- From my mother, "Bobby (her fiance) has died of a massive heart attack."

I braced myself for what was to come as I slid the answer icon over and handed the phone to David. "Hello?" I couldn't hear what his dad was saying, but I knew it wasn't good. His mother was recovering

3 LEADING WITH JESUS

from a stomach virus, so my first thought was that she was sicker. Or I thought it could be related to his elderly grandmother, who had been transported earlier in the week to a new nursing home facility after a brief hospital stay.

It took me a few minutes to realize it was neither of these scenarios. It had something to do with our business, and it wasn't good. I could hear the "Oh," and the "Hmmm," grunts of concern and piece it all together. Our state had experienced significant rainfall, and the flood waters had violently invaded our store.

THE FLOOD

Leaks in the building were commonplace as our roof was old and deteriorating. We had attempted to fix spots here and there, but thirty thousand square feet is a lot of roof and a lot of cash out the door. Cash we didn't have. David's dad has always been such a dedicated soul. He was concerned about the torrential downpours and roof leaks and had made his way over to the store in the wee hours of the morning to check the buckets which were set up to catch the minor ceiling leaks. He had no idea he would find the city's water pumps had not functioned properly causing water to rapidly take over our spaces. Granted, heavy rains had spread throughout our community. However, instead of getting a couple of inches of water due to the rains, we received much more due to a faulty drainage system. In a matter of 45 minutes, two feet of water filled our floors, which held hundreds of thousands of dollars worth of what was now ruined ribbon, florals, home decor and other items.

My husband threw some clothes on and headed out the door to inspect the damages, but not before he knelt beside our bed, grabbed my hand and led us in prayer. He also gave me a pep talk assuring me it was all going to be okay and God was going to take care of this situation. As I heard his tires leave our gravel driveway, all I could do was pray and ask God to help us and to keep him safe in his journey into the unknown. David called me on the way to let me know about the dangerous road conditions. When he arrived, he called me again. I could tell by the sound of his voice it was bad — really, really bad.

The situation was worse than we had imagined. Our parking lot was covered in water, he reported. The water rose chest deep in some areas. One of our delivery trucks was submerged with only the cab barely visible. I was determined to stay positive and upbeat, but he sent me pictures of the beautiful interior of our store covered in nasty, sewer-ridden, murky water. As I looked at the pictures, a river of tears began to flow, just like the water flowing through our store.

I wasn't crying because I doubted God or His goodness. I wasn't crying because of what we had lost. I was grieving all of the hard work and sacrifices made for years to get our business to where it was. I looked again at the picture of our warehouse. It was a graveyard of toppled over cardboard boxes amounting to the hundreds. The same boxes that once held our livelihood now held wet and dirty flowers, muddy ribbon, filthy snowman tree toppers, and ruined faux moss reindeer.

When this catastrophic event occurred, both of our businesses were in good places. We had an amazing retail staff, who were moving and shaking. They had worked so hard to pretty up the place for spring by boxing up out-of-season merchandise, putting out new merchandise, and organizing everything. The day prior to the flood, our wholesale staff spent the entire day planning and vision casting for the new year. We had plans to recruit new customers, improve customer service, clean up our warehouse, and strengthen our sales. Everyone was fired up and ready to take the business to the next level.

To say we were disappointed would be an understatement. How in the world were we going to move forward from this event? Our main concern was our employees. We wanted them to be able to have a

3 LEADING WITH JESUS

place to come to work and get paid. Our main goal was for no one to miss a paycheck. We weren't sure how it was going to work out, but we knew God would take care of us. Many people, along the way, were telling us to let people go or lay them off to save money. But we didn't feel that was what God wanted for us. We prayed for him to make a way for us to keep all of our staff and to pay them for their labor.

Part of our mission in being Jesus in the marketplace is to trust Him in the good and the bad. This was definitely bad, but we made a decision when we first heard the news to count it all a joy. We decided if one person's life could be pointed to Jesus through this event all of our temporary pain and discouragement was worth it.

The concept of profiting from our trials is illustrated in James 1:2-3, *"My brethren, count it all joy when you fall into various trials, knowing that the testing of your faith produces patience."* Let's pause there a minute. We definitely felt like we were in a trial, and I, personally, knew I could use more patience. So far, so good. The verse goes on to say, *"But let patience have its perfect work, that you may be perfect and complete, lacking nothing."* (James 1:4) Wow! So maybe we will be made perfect through this trial. I wouldn't mind being made perfect, Lord. I don't know if perfection on earth is attainable, but it seems the only way to find out is to go through a lot of trials. Perfection still seems an impossible feat, but at this point, we were game for trying.

The lesson doesn't stop there, the verses go on to say, *"If any of you lack wisdom, let him ask God, who gives to all liberally and without reproach, and it will be given to him. But let him ask in faith, with no doubt, for he who doubts is like a wave of the sea driven and tossed by the wind. For let not that man suppose that he will receive anything from the Lord; he is a double-minded man, unstable in all his ways."* (James 1:5-8).

This verse seemed to fit our situation so well. We were definitely going to need the wisdom of the Lord in order to move forward and accomplish His will and purpose. We also realized this was one of those times our faith was going to have to be big. We couldn't doubt, because the word plainly told us not to doubt or we would be classified as "double-minded" and "unstable" in all of our ways. Those were two descriptions we didn't want attached to us.

That cold day in February, I sent out a text to our team, complete with pictures of inside the store, to let them know about our situation, but I took the time to reassure them and encourage them of God's goodness. We explained to our people we weren't going to let this situation get us down and we communicated a message of hope. We were simply trying to do what Jesus would do. We let them know we would keep in touch and relay information as we were able. We wanted to be transparent with them. We shared how much we cared about them and our goals were to be operating as soon as possible. We asked them to pray with us in the days and months to come.

The attitude of a team usually trickles down from the leaders in charge of the team. It's almost like parenting or babysitting. Have you ever watched a child get hurt and the mother or caregiver begins to freak out causing the child to freak out? I remember my mom telling me when I was a new mom to remain calm when my child was hurt or sick and my child would remain calm. The same concept applies to leading a team. If you panic, they will panic. If you complain and whine, they will complain and whine. If you are positive and upbeat, nine times out of ten, your team members will be as well. You must remain honest, but positive and hopeful in the face of both small and giant setbacks. You have to call out negativity and redirect the words of those around you to be words that build up. I remember an instance when a team member made a negative remark a few days after the flood, "We are never going to get this cleaned up." I stopped the team member, "We aren't going to talk like that. We are going to get this cleaned up. And we have to be careful what words we speak over

3 LEADING WITH JESUS

this situation." Did I feel the same way she did about never getting the mess cleaned up? Sure, it was a natural response. But I made a decision to not give in to the natural, but to power through with the supernatural help of the Lord.

We cannot control other people's behaviors or emotions, no matter how good and effective we are as leaders. There are some people who will choose to be negative, no matter how positive and encouraging you are to them. I remember the sting of the comments some of our customers made at our flood sale, where we were attempting to sell anything we could in order to survive the ordeal. One lady remarked, "I'm glad this happened so I could get some deals." I am pretty sure my jaw almost hit the sidewalk. But people like this are not usually the majority, so you can't let them get the best of you and drag you down. Sadly, sometimes ignorance rears its ugly head in situations like these, and we have to let it go keeping our focus on the finish line.

FACE THE MESS WITHOUT COMPLAINING

Within a few hours after being informed of the devastation, I found myself at our store in my waders. Normally, I only wear them when trout fishing in North Carolina with David and our family. I never expected to wear them to work! I had decided to do a Facebook Live video to share our news with our customers. We wanted them to know what we were facing. A lot of times on social media, it is easy to only portray the good and exciting news. It's harder to be vulnerable and share disappointments, but we didn't want to pretend we weren't going through a hard time. We used this hard time as an opportunity to share our faith in God and His goodness.

As I made my way through the water, which had receded from knee-deep to mid-calf, I told our customers we refused to complain or be disappointed. I shared with them how we had so much to be

DISAPPOINTMENTS AND SETBACKS

grateful for, while pointing out that certain items were still okay. I used my head lamp as a guide to spotlight the items that were lost while telling our audience we chose to believe Romans 8:28. *"And we know that in all things God works for the good of those who love him, who have been called according to his purpose."*

We also chose to believe God would restore to us what was lost. We were reminded of the story of Job who had everything taken from him, not only his wife and children, but livestock as well. Even covered in boils, Job never stopped praising God. At least we didn't have it as bad as poor Job. Can you imagine suffering his losses and still praising God through it all? God knew Job would choose to continue to praise Him. Satan just thought he knew more than the Almighty. Rest assured, God always has the upper hand in your situation.

If you find yourself going through a trial, remember the advice of Paul in Philippians 3:14: *"Do all things without complaining and disputing, that you may become blameless and harmless, children of God without fault in the midst of a crooked and perverse generation, among whom you shine as lights in the world, holding fast the word of life, so that I may rejoice in the day of Christ that I have not run in vain or labored in vain."*

There are people in the world who don't know of Job and his story, but they know us and our story. You have a chance to live like Job facing trial after trial with confidence, grace and mercy, just like Jesus did, time and time again. You may be the only glimpse of love and hope a person sees, and you can't win your battles by whining and complaining. Our pastor, Bobby Gourley, put it this way, "Complaining about the ways of God robs us of obtaining the promises of God. Complaining makes us the victim and destroys our testimony."

Did you catch that? Complaining destroys your testimony, which is not what you want to do when attempting to live for Christ, showing His love and hope to our broken and hurting world. You have to make up your mind every day to not complain. Are you going to be perfect?

3 LEADING WITH JESUS

Probably not. You will fail and find yourself grumbling now and again, but what if you could significantly cut back on the amount of times you respond negatively to setbacks? If you are living your life filled with complaints, Paul's word in Philippians says you are laboring in vain. I don't know about you, but I don't want all of this to be for naught. It all goes back to your "Why." I want to make a difference for Jesus in the lives of those around me, don't you? You are called to be a light, and you need your light to shine brightest during your darkest moments. And believe me when I say, people are watching you in your darkest moments. They need to see you practice what you preach. Words aren't as effective as actions.

The book of Joel says, *"I will repay you for the years the locusts have eaten—the great locust and the young locust, the other locusts and the locust swarm—my great army that I sent out among you. You will have plenty to eat, until you are full, and you will praise the name of the Lord your God, who has worked wonders for you; never again will my people be shamed"* (Joel 2:25-26). When we found ourselves face-to-face with the locusts, we were also face-to-face with the decision to trust. It was totally up to God to redeem our business. We boldly went to His throne and told him so. Maybe there is something in your life you need to go to the throne with emboldened with faith and expecting God for the answer.

I remember the first time my attention was drawn to a passage in Isaiah, *"When the enemy shall come in like a flood, the Spirit of the Lord shall lift up a standard against him"* (Isaiah 59:19). Yes, Lord! Can I get an amen? Maybe you aren't facing a flood, but I know you are facing, or have faced something similar, if you've lived more than a few years. God doesn't take the attacks of the enemy lightly. His word encourages us, *"If you are willing and obedient, you shall eat the good of the land; but if you refuse and rebel, you shall be eaten by the sword; for the mouth of the Lord has spoken"* (Isaiah 1:19). This verse doesn't tell us we might eat or we could eat or we should eat, it says you SHALL eat of the good of the land. Eating from the good of the land is inevitable, no matter what our physical eyes can see, when we follow God's path and plan.

During the days following our massive flood, we thought of all of the wonders God had done in our business and in our lives, and as we did, the disappointments we were facing started to feel a little smaller and smaller, as God was magnified more and more. As we shared these messages with our customers and team members, we took the first steps toward recovery by glorifying God, praising Him in the storm, lifting our arms in worship, and showering Him with thanksgiving, all the while asking and expecting Him to meet our needs.

Each day we shared social media updates of the hundreds of volunteers that showed up with food, cleaning supplies, words of encouragement and working hands. We were thankful. And not just on a surface level, but we were indebted to them with deep, soul level gratitude.

Gratitude can take us such a long way. As I mentioned earlier, I make lists of all of the things I have to be thankful for during the disappointments. On this particular day, I was thankful my husband and children were all alive and well. When I stopped to think about it, their well-being was what was most important. I thought about the people in the neighborhood behind our store who were being forced out of their homes and having their animals picked up by the local animal control in order to keep them safe during the rising waters. I also thought about people in other parts of the state who had lost their lives in the flooding. I play the "it can always be worse" game a lot. It helps ground me and give me a fresh outlook.

THE PROMISE

I also focused on the story of Noah. If God could keep Noah and

3 LEADING WITH JESUS

his family safe and eventually bring them to dry ground, He could definitely do the same for our family and our employees. I tried to look past the water and see the rainbow that was coming. We have to expect the rainbow after our storms. We have to focus on the bright colors of His promises. *"I have set my rainbow in the clouds, and it will be the sign of the covenant between me and the earth"* (Genesis 9:13). Although we were inconvenienced for a period of time due to the flood, our hopes were not drowned by the rain no matter how relentless, pelting, and hopeless each drop felt as it attempted to pierce our hearts and steal our joy.

Knowing and focusing on the fact we have a Saviour who loves us and promises us a home in heaven helped us deal with the disappointments brought by this event, as well as all of the other setbacks we encountered before this occasion. Looking back at God's track record clearly reveals His faithful character. He is our Redeemer, Restorer and Healer.

When you choose an attitude of praise in spite of your circumstances, people take notice. They begin to watch you. You are given the opportunity to show your team, and those in your circle of influence, what it's like to walk something out with Jesus by your side. The world desperately needs to see more Christ-bearers remaining faithful to Jesus during the storms. Every comment you make has the ability to set the atmosphere. Throughout the flood event, whenever I heard someone make a negative comment, I was quick to say, "We are going to think positively and say good things." This is all part of a leader's duty to protect the culture and the vision.

Most days, we had local news agencies contacting us for interviews. It's a blur how many interviews we have done regarding the flood. But each time, it is up to us to let our joy shine. God was using our story to show his redemptive power – to ultimately get out His story of mercy and power. We were willing to be used as the cover.

DISAPPOINTMENTS AND SETBACKS 3

The Bible tells us the power of life and death is held in our tongues (Proverbs 18:21). In the days that followed the great flood, we put in our best efforts to remain upbeat and positive. We continued to create many social media posts of our team smiling, dancing and working their hearts out to clean, salvage and restore. The days were long, the work was dirty, and we gave our all to the wet building which was slowly getting more and more stinky from the mold and mildew. We lost over a quarter of a million dollars in products. We had flood insurance, but not everything was covered in our policy. As mentioned previously, our main concern from day one was our team. We wanted them to be okay. We wanted to make sure they were paid even if we were not. One week, payroll was approaching, and we were about $3,000 short of having enough money to pay everyone. Without sales coming in, times were tough. A few days before we had to turn our payroll numbers into our accountant, David and I got a sweet card in the mail with a check made out to us in the amount of $3,000. I was blown away at God's faithfulness and astounded at the obedience of the family who sent us the check. Everyone was paid. I slept a little easier that night.

GOD GIVES US WHO WE NEED

I remember one day saying, "Hmmm. God, we have a great team. It's healthy and happy. We are all at a good and comfortable place with one another. Why would this happen to us now?" A light bulb went off in my head as the Holy Spirit said, "That's why you have the team you have now. I knew who you would need for this, and I brought them to you." Several of the people working for us during the flood had ministry in their hearts. They saw our business as their personal mission, volunteering for more time than we could pay them, leaving us overwhelmed with gratitude. Some even recruited friends to join in our clean-up efforts.

3 LEADING WITH JESUS

Our store was flooded a second time, but this time it was a flood of volunteers to help us. A few of the volunteers were from the surrounding neighborhood that had also experienced flood damage. They showed up to help us because they loved our store. Many of our volunteers came from our church. It was amazing and humbling. Every ounce of pride we had was swallowed on day two or three when we realized there was no possible way we could pay back all the people who had offered their time and energy to work in soaking wet cardboard, ruined merchandise, and cold temperatures, as our heating unit was not working at the time. It's during those moments when you truly begin to see the fruits of being Jesus in the marketplace. People helped us because they loved us and had compassion in their hearts for us. They helped us, we believe, because God sent them there. He is where our help comes from, but I know he likes to use people to be His hands and feet.

We have to trust God above all else. I remember all the times we struggled financially and David would say, "It's okay, Jen, we will be okay. Worst case scenario, we sell off all of our inventory, pay off our debt, and get out of this business. We're good." Never in a million years did we think our inventory would be lost in flood waters. We would have been better off financially, better prepared, had it happened to be a fire, but we were not prepared for this flood. Our insurance adjuster even told us, "You can't prepare for this kind of thing. You have to take it day by day." We realized we had been trusting in our inventory, and not in the God who gave us the inventory. In some respects you could say that the flood was a blessing because it caused us to re-center our trust in God. It may seem crazy to be willing to experience monumental losses in order to gain more trust in God, but when our relationship with Jesus takes the driver seat in our lives the payoff is greater than anything we can imagine. But we have to allow him to be in the driver's seat and not just a co-pilot.

We have to reach for the future, while learning from the past. As Paul said, *"I press on toward the goal for the prize of the upward call of God in Christ Jesus"* (Philippians 3:14). A "Pollyanna" attitude isn't realistic for most of us in leadership. We can't just pretend everything is right and fair in the world, but we do have a prize waiting for us at the end of our lives when we live for Jesus and finish well. *"For this world is not our permanent home; we are looking forward to a home yet to come"* (Hebrews 13:14).

Now that some time has passed, we are able to talk a little more lightheartedly about the flood and the damage it caused. So many conversations start with, "Before the flood…." or "Well, that was pre-flood days." We sometimes laugh, throwing the hashtag symbol in the air at one another while saying, "#floodapocalypse2019" or "#floodhappens." While we may laugh about floods happening, we also know God happens, and when He happens, there's nothing He can't do. We all are full of hope and excitement for what the future holds for us as we renovate and rebuild.

The good thing about disappointments and setbacks is they are not permanent when we seek God first and depend upon Him. Setbacks are a part of our story. Sometimes they are a sentence in the story, and sometimes, like you find in this book, there's a whole chapter dedicated to a setback because of its defining properties. The good news is we get to choose how our setbacks and disappointments define us. Are we going to wallow in self-pity, get angry, give up and quit? Or are we going to raise our arms in victory, sword in hand and charge into the battle as a member of the army of the Lord? I can let you in on a little secret: the latter is how you win the victory and send the enemy fleeing.

3 LEADING WITH JESUS

EXERCISE

1. What has been a setback, disappointment or defining moment in your marriage, parenting, or business? Spend some time talking to the Lord about it to ensure you are carrying the right attitude about the situation. Ask Him to heal you if you still harbor resentment and bitterness, or if you have lost your hope.

2. Allow the Holy Spirit to empower you as you define yourself by who you are in Christ and not who you are based on your circumstances.

3. Practice positive affirmation. What negative statements have you been speaking into existence over your life, family, friends, workplace and world? Recognize these statements and cut them out of your speech patterns. When you catch yourself saying things like, "Well, that was bound to happen," or "If something bad is going to happen, it's going to happen to me," stop yourself and replace them with statements like: "Through God nothing is impossible," and "I am blessed and highly favored. I am a child of the Most High God. The same power which coursed through the veins of Jesus still courses through my veins today. I am the head and not the tail."

Chapter Four

VISION CASTING AND CULTURE BUILDING

Vision is defined by the Google dictionary as, "The ability to think about or plan for the future using imagination or wisdom. "When vision is lacking, there is no clear direction of where anyone is going. Having a vision helps to ensure your success. George Washington Carver put it this way, "Where there is no vision, there is no hope." Proverbs 29:18 tells us, *"Where there is no prophetic vision, the people cast off restraint."* In other words, they perish. If you don't have a clear vision, the people under your leadership will operate according to their own vision. Before you know it, everyone will be doing their own thing and going in multiple directions instead of working toward a common goal.

To determine your vision, you must first assess your values, set goals and establish steps to accomplish those goals. Vision involves forward thinking, looking into the future to see the big picture and establishing time frames of when you want to be where you want to be. Once you have determined your vision, it is your job to communicate your vision to your team. You must have buy-in from them in order to be successful. If your employees are not on board with your vision, or if they don't know what your vision is, your goals will never be achieved. They will begin to take liberties in how the ship

4 LEADING WITH JESUS

is steered, adjusting the sails little by little, until you are off course.

Vision is not just about long-term planning; it involves daily activities. If people don't know what is expected of them each day, they won't know what you want from them over time. Establishing daily, monthly, and yearly goals is critical to your success and theirs.

In order to gain buy-in from your team members, you need goals bigger than yourselves. Most employees aren't interested in putting more money in the business owners' pockets. However, nearly all people are driven by a need to feel they are sowing into something bigger than themselves. On that note, it's important for businesses to have a cause they support. For example, we help support a women's clinic in our area that teaches pregnant women about Jesus and gives them the resources they need to prepare for and keep their unplanned babies. We also support our church's local Dream Center, which provides food and life skills to people in need. Recently, we have added an additional international cause. We will be sending one employee, per year, on a mission trip to Chapel Haiti, where orphans are educated, clothed, and fed. The more sales we generate, the more we are able to give to these causes, and both customers and employees are often excited about sowing into visions that strengthen the local community and the world.

In its simplest form your leadership and business vision should include being Jesus in the marketplace, which is similar to "The Why" we covered in the first chapter. Of course, you can have other visions, as well. But when we seek kingdom things first, everything else falls into place. (Matthew 6:33)

LAYING GROUNDWORK

When we interview candidates for positions, we always tell them about our vision for the company. We explain the company culture and communicate our desire to be a positive, fun, committed and driven workplace. We also explain daily workloads and our desire to know one another and foster a genuine sense of community. We share our values, such as our goal to be a place that honors and respects all people. It's important employees know from the get-go we maintain an atmosphere where people work together to resolve problems without resorting to abusive language and negative attitudes.

Oftentimes new hires may be standoffish because of previous job experiences that were negative. Most people carry emotional baggage from one job to the next unaware they might be projecting things onto people who are not responsible for their hurt. Unfortunately, not everyone wants a positive workplace. I know that thought may sound crazy, but there are people who love gossip, and prefer a low standard, minimal effort workplace. They can thrive on drama. They have let the storms of life get inside of them while they are inside of the storms causing them to be poisonous to everyone in their paths. Some people don't want to be held accountable, or be like Jesus, so it's best for them to know the expectations on the front end.

Once an employee is hired, our Employee Handbook reiterates to them how we do business. Here is our welcome statement:

"Welcome! We are thrilled to have you as a part of our team. We value all people and make it a priority to treat our employees with respect and honor.

It's important to us that we equip you with the tools you need to be successful. Here, you will receive training that will build your skill set and make you a valuable employee in any workplace. However, our goal is to treat you so well that you won't ever want to leave. After all, our employees are an integral part of our success.

In the event that a problem arises, we ask that you speak to a member of management immediately. Our Human Resources Department maintains an open door policy, and no concern is too small to bring to the attention of a manager. We are also open to suggestions for change and always welcome your feedback. Thank

4 LEADING WITH JESUS

you!"

Every place of employment has a culture, whether it is spelled out in an employee handbook or not. It is up to the leaders of the organization to cast the vision for the workplace culture and help team members carry it out. While much has been written and researched about developing successful workplace cultures, in my experience, a good workplace culture is an atmosphere in which employees:

- Work together to achieve shared goals
- Display positive attitudes as a result of feeling valued
- Receive opportunities to grow in their knowledge and skills through training

Negative attitudes in the workplace spread like wildfire, especially if management is the source of the negativity. On that note, the longer someone works for a company, the more he/she is looked to as the person in charge or the person with authority. Thus, it's important to make sure people with seniority are leading well whether they have an official leadership title or not. As the old idiom goes, "One bad apple can spoil the bunch." We have learned this to be true in our workplace. It only takes one person to pollute and dilute the culture you have worked so hard to create. It only takes one person to start a new but bad habit. The French proverb tells us, "Rome wasn't built in a day." Your workplace culture won't be either.

In today's culture, everything is blamed on leadership. While I tend to agree that a lot of what goes wrong in an organization does fall on the leaders shoulders, it is unrealistic to expect round-the-clock perfection from yourself and employees. Whenever a disaster unfolds at work, I ask myself if something could have been done differently by the leaders involved to avoid the incident. Sometimes, the answer is yes and I make a note of what happened and how we can improve next time. Then, I move on. I also help my team move on after a negative incident. If you and your team members are learning from mistakes and taking proactive approaches to success the next go around, be assured that you are on the right track. Conversely, if you are living in the past, and always ruminating about past mistakes, you are fostering a toxic atmosphere. Mistakes and failures are a part of life and business. It's not a question of if they will happen, but when. How you handle mistakes impacts employees and your workplace culture.

I will admit I hate seeing memes on social media pointing the fingers at leaders with wording which speaks in absolutes. For example, "People don't leave bad jobs, they leave bad people." Really? I don't buy it. Granted, there are a lot of times people leave people, but sometimes people leave because leaders have prayed them away. Or maybe management was putting pressure on them to actually do their job. Or because God has something better in store for the person leaving. We have to be willing to question our leadership, but it's not always about us, as leaders. The sooner we realize it, the easier we can sleep at night.

THE STORY OF SODOM

There's a biblical story that demonstrates the importance of taking stock of the culture in which you are operating. In the story, two strangers walked into a city they had never visited. A gentleman met them in the town square and invited the men to come to his home. While the new strangers were inside the gentleman's home, they heard a disturbance outside. Upon investigating the source, the men inside discovered the house was surrounded by other men, young and old alike, on all sides. The men outside called out to the homeowner, "Send out the men that are inside. We want to have sex with them."

4 LEADING WITH JESUS

    The city in which this story takes place is Sodom, and the men described as visitors were angels disguised as men. Sodom was a desperately wretched city, drowning in sin and darkness. Abraham and Lot had to split up, because the land they both occupied was having difficulty sustaining both of their families. Genesis 13:8-13 tells us Lot chose to move his family to the twin cities of Sodom and Gomorrah. Lot was said to have chosen Sodom and Gomorrah because of its fertile ground and beauty. Due to the beauty of the cities, Lot seemingly overlooked the sin taking place within its walls. Even though he knew first hand of the sin taking place, he remained in its dysfunctional culture long after arriving. He found it difficult to give up his life in the cities and follow the voice of the Lord, despite its rapidly decaying culture. Part of his reason for staying had to do with his wife wanting to stay. But God had something better in store for Lot and his family. They couldn't see it and instead lingered in a place they did not belong.

    It's easy for us to do this in our workplace culture, as well. We become comfortable in the bed in which we lie. We don't want to obey God and move in a different direction, because we have grown accustomed to our place. Maybe we listen to outside influences telling us that it's good enough or that we can't expect change considering the staff we have. Perhaps, we don't feel like we have the energy to change after all of the hours we have put in as leaders. When you find yourself snuggled deep into the smothering blankets of comfort, it can become difficult to overcome your own selfish wants and needs and recognize that God is speaking to you to move your organization in a different direction. Maybe God wants the people in your organization to be held to a higher standard showing more honor and respect for one another. Perhaps He wants you to work a little harder for unity even if it means a difficult conversation. If we live with our heads in the sand, we may have an "I just can't deal" attitude where ignoring someone's bad attitude or turning a blind eye to the way an associate talked to a customer or pretending not to notice when someone breaks a rule becomes commonplace.

In Sodom and Gomorrah, God told Lot, *"Flee for your lives! Don't look back, and don't stop anywhere in the plain! Flee to the mountains or you will be swept away!"* (Genesis 19:17) But Lot's wife looked back, and she became a pillar of salt. (Genesis 19:26). God wants to do a new thing in your business culture. He wants to focus on what is in front of you instead of what is behind you. Change can be hard, but creating a culture in the workplace that honors Him and His flock will be worth the time you take to make it happen.

I have read a lot of quotes about how the rear view mirror is smaller than the windshield for a reason. I find this quote to have a biblical basis. In Luke 17:30-33, Jesus talks about the coming of the kingdom of God, *"Likewise, no one in the field should go back for anything. Remember Lot's wife."* Moving forward to cast a vision and build a culture is difficult. Yes, you should learn from your past mistakes, but there are things you shouldn't dwell on. Like Lot's wife, we become immovable pillars when we become set in our ways, not wanting to change, and pining for the past. We must think, look and walk forward in order to move toward the culture we want to create within our organization.

ACCOUNTABLE LOVE

An employee told me, "You are the kind of boss who keeps us accountable, but we know you love us." I was so happy to hear she had caught the vision for our culture. Another said, "Thanks for always checking in and making sure I'm okay." This particular team member actually thanked me for the correction I gave her about her increased tardiness. Sometimes there is a legitimate reason for an employee's behavior. And if we want to lead differently than the world, it is worth the time to check in and follow up.

4 LEADING WITH JESUS

Most people want to be held to an achievable standard. People need and crave boundaries. As a leader, we must be willing and able to set boundaries for them. Defining boundaries is easy, enforcing them is necessary but difficult. Boundaries are a part of the culture we should all strive to create in our lives and in our workplace. Leading intentionally takes effort. It doesn't come naturally for most people. It means taking time to get to know your team members, and finding out their strengths and weaknesses. Find out what your people love to do, and make every effort to put them in a place that uses their strengths. For example, one employee loved entering new products into our point-of-sale system. I assumed everyone disliked doing it, because I heard so much grumbling about it from other team members. When I realized it was something she loved, I assigned her to enter all new products, and she was happy with her new role.

You can't assume you know what people like to do. And you can't assume that just because a person is good at a particular task he or she must love to do that task. Let's be real, though. You can't always let Mary Sue do everything she loves and nothing she loathes. Your business would not be successful. That's not reality, and I am not suggesting you do so. However, take some time to get to know your employees' strengths. Every summer, I take each of my female associates to lunch to spend one on one time with them. I use this time to check in and see how things are going, but it's also an informal way to gain insight into job satisfaction. Whether over lunch or during a performance evaluation, ask your people what they really enjoy doing and find out what they wished they didn't have to do. You may find, like I did, one employee loves to do what another dislikes. Letting your team members know you care about their happiness and success on the job is part of building a positive culture. People always appreciate the opportunity to provide feedback on the job they do day in and day out.

At work, we have an "Awesome Box." The box has an opening big enough for an index card to slip through. The sign on the front reads, "Caught You Being Awesome." The purpose of the box is for team members to write notes about one another and drop them inside. During our staff meetings, I read the notes aloud for everyone to hear. Most of the time, the notes are anonymous, so the team members don't know who gave the compliment, although they can usually guess. This simple activity builds community and morale. Everyone is smiling. I try to make sure everyone in the room has a card in the box at the start of each meeting. Even if the person has been frustrating your team and not doing the best job, it's important to know you tried to encourage your team members and did everything in your power to make their work atmosphere one in which they can thrive.

Your daily interactions with people can help them to get to know you. People are rarely fooled about who cares for them and who doesn't. As hard as we try, it's difficult to hide your true feelings about others. It can come out in a joke or a moment of frustration, but it will come out. For this reason, it is so important that you show the people around you how much you appreciate their efforts. It makes it much easier to discipline people when they know you care. Think about the times you have been disciplined in your life. Did anyone ever fool you? Did you take criticism better from someone you knew cared, verses someone who made you feel like a means to an end? Try to put yourself in the shoes of your people and remember what it felt like when you weren't the one in charge.

FIGHT FOR A JESUS CULTURE

Remember, not everyone working for you is going to buy into your vision. Some people aren't called to help you fulfill your vision and mission. It's important to remember some people show up just for a paycheck. They may even do an excellent job, but they are incapable of looking at the work the way you look at the work. Maybe you are

4 LEADING WITH JESUS

a stopping point in their journey and not their final destination. The sooner you can accept the fact not all people will treat your business as their own, the more peace you can experience.

Be mindful of the culture you are building every day. Set goals for yourself and your business on how you want things to run. Don't settle, and please don't let one or two naysayers change your culture. You have to fight for your culture. Take ownership of the atmosphere. Become a warrior willing to fight the hard battles for your team, for yourself, and for Jesus. You have to have conversations with people letting them know what they are doing to disrupt the culture. For example, "In this company, we take ownership of our mistakes without casting the blame on someone else," or "We work as a team. No one person can make this place run. It takes all of us. You are not in competition with anyone here but yourself."

Ask yourself, what conclusions do you want people to draw about your business when joining your team? What do you hope they say about your team when they leave? The same principles that apply to your workplace culture also apply with your customers. Customers can't be fooled any more than team members can. They know if you truly care about them, or if you are only focused on making the next sale and getting from them whatever you can get. Building relationships with your coworkers, managers, and employees is a very important step in the achievement of the workplace lifestyle you wish to achieve.

As discussed previously, another part of your culture involves praying for your team members and customers. It is commonplace for us to stop and pray for someone who is having a hard day, or once they leave the store. We even like to send our customers cards or small gifts when we know one of them has had surgery, a death, or a hard time. One simple heartfelt prayer or card can make the difference in helping someone feel valued and cared about. Taking care of people (His Father's business) was a top priority of Jesus. Customers have a choice of where to do business, and we want them to do business with us because of how they are treated as soon as they walk into the door. We strive to provide Jesus level customer service.

HONOR THOSE YOU SERVE

With brick and mortar stores closing at a rapid pace, we have to do something to be set apart. We take time to get to know the names and stories of our customers. We also provide them with human experiences they can't get online. People always remember how you made them feel.

Many customer service books reiterate that the customer is always right. But if we are honest, we will admit we don't believe that statement to be 100 percent true. We do give our customers the benefit of the doubt, but we also need to make good business decisions. There have been instances in our business where our customers didn't agree with our return policy or other practices. In these cases, we have to be secure in how we are operating. People outside the business don't always have all the pieces of the puzzle to know why you do what you do. There will always be people who don't agree with us. For this reason, it is even more important for us to get to know our clients. When they know us and trust us, they will, in turn, give us the benefit of the doubt in sticky situations. And as you know by now, leadership is full of sticky situations.

ONE PERCENT

About 50 percent of people won't care about your culture. It's not out of spite; they are simply not invested, involved or interested in what you are doing. Another 49 percent of people do care about what you are trying to accomplish. They believe in you and want to see you succeed. Then, there's the one percent who are against you,

4 LEADING WITH JESUS

and find fault with everything you do. These people aren't interested in encouraging you or building you up. I learned this principle from a speech given by, now retired, Mayor Bobby Irons. I have remembered this illustration time and time again when it seems everyone is working against me.

There have been so many nights I have lain in bed in tears or distress because of the one percent. I have let them get to me. I have had to pray and read God's word to get back to a healthy place. Over time, I have learned to not let the voices of the one percent be louder than the forty-nine percent. Romans 12:2 tells us, *"Do not be conformed to this world, but be transformed by the renewal of your mind, that by testing you may discern what is the will of God, what is good and acceptable and perfect."* The world is going to have an opinion about you and your leadership, especially if you are trying to lead with Jesus. But God's voice has to be number one. It has to be the loudest, because it is the truest. The fastest way to get yourself down (and those around you down) is to forget who you are in Christ and to forget who you are working for in your marketplace. The fastest way to build yourself, your vision and your culture, as a leader, is to remind yourself of what God says about you.

I realize I may sound like a broken record at this point in the book with the number of times I have suggested reading God's word. But His Word truly holds the answer to all of your questions. Start reading His Word and learning what He says He wants for you. Your vision and mission need to match His vision and mission for your life and business. If you don't know where to start, remember the great commission:

"Therefore go and make disciples of all the nations, baptizing them in the name of the Father and the Son and the Holy Spirit, and teaching them to obey everything I have commanded you. And surely I am with you always, to the very end of the age." (Matthew 28:19-20)

VISION CASTING AND CULTURE BUILDING

Start each day looking for opportunities to fulfill the Great Commission. Mission trips are amazing, but you don't have to go to the ends of the earth to share Jesus with your community. Whenever we face trials and tribulations, we reread our vision statement, "To be Jesus in the marketplace." Doing so enables us to gain perspective on next steps. Finally, focus your thoughts and actions on building a culture based on engagement, respect, authenticity, grace, mercy, love, input, accountability and correction. Remember, visions aren't just for the workplace; they are for every aspect of your life.

EXERCISE

1. What kind of culture do you want to create in your workplace?

2. What is your vision for your organization? Make sure you take the time to draft your vision statement. Filter all of your decisions through this vision. For example, if you are considering offering a new service or product to your clients, process it through your vision to make sure it fits. This will save you time and energy as your vision will answer most of the questions for you.

3. What kind of culture do you want to create in your home?

4. What is your vision for your family?

5. Consider creating a vision board to help visualize where you are and where you're going. It should represent your dreams, goals, and ways you want to help those around you.

Chapter Five

IF GOD WANTS ME TO BE SUCCESSFUL, WHY IS IT SO HARD?

If God wants me to be successful, why is it so hard? Have you ever asked yourself that question? If you've ever experienced difficulties while trying to do good, I am sure the thought has crossed your mind. I promised you we would get back to this subject. It's a question I asked my husband before I joined the business, and it's a question I wrestled with a lot along the way especially after the tragedy of losing so much in the flood. A couple of years prior to the flood, David and I got one piece of bad news after another creating a string of frustration and disheartened demeanors.

Paul's words came to me, *"Therefore do not lose heart. Even though our outward man is perishing, yet the inward man is being renewed each day."* 2 Corinthians 4:16

But sometimes, it's hard not to lose heart. It's really hard. Especially when we don't feel the renewing of our inner man. The bills are piling up, the people aren't cooperating, the building has maintenance issues needing attention, and the computer system promising to change your life for the better is malfunctioning causing you to come close to just running away.

5 LEADING WITH JESUS

It's during these times we must pray and seek God for revelation. Revelation is always on the other side of prayer. While seeking Him, I have realized what we think success looks like may not line up with what God sees as us being successful. For us, as small business owners, it may seem to come in the form of sales, receiving merchandise on time, financial blessings, or finding the right products and employees.

God reminds me often that He is more interested in my development and spiritual growth than He is my finances and things being easy. He wants us to depend on Him, keep talking to Him, keep believing and trusting Him to make us successful in ways which matter. The American dream is misleading. Job 14:1 speaks to me, *"Man who is born of woman is few of days and full of trouble."* People feel entitled to happiness, but neither the U.S. Constitution nor the Bible promises us happiness. The Constitution promises us the pursuit of happiness. The Bible promises us an abundant life. Some may look at the word abundant and mentally define it as having nice things, a terrific job, and unfailing health. Maybe life isn't about the American dream, a perfect marriage, lovely children, and a white picket fence. Developing God sized dreams involves developing a dependence on Him which is ultimately a gift to us. God's dreams for us strengthen us, help us to run good races, fight the good fight and magnify His name in all we do. It seems to me we should be more about a God dream. We have heaven to gain. God sized dreams don't always come packaged in sunshine yellow wrapping paper and a sparkly bow. Usually, they look more like something handed to you in a used, crumpled grocery sack. However, what's inside of a God sized dream is more lasting and meaningful than the packaging. It has an eternal value beyond imagination.

DEEP ROOTS

Pastor Lee Cummings once prophesied over me saying, "God has given you deep roots. Roots grow deeper during the dry seasons. And God is aware of your dry seasons. God acknowledges that things have been hard for you, and He wants you to know the reason your journey has looked different than some others is because His purpose for you is unique and different from others."

This prophetic word was given at the perfect time. We needed encouragement as we were almost drowning in feelings of despair, wringing our hands trying to figure out what to do next. Prophesy should always be confirmation to us and not revelation. After all, why would God tell someone else something instead of me if I am asking, tuned in and listening. David and I had been seeking the Lord and asking Him to please tell us what we needed to do after the flood. Do we press on? Do we give up and do something different with our careers and ministry? We didn't want to miss him. On the same night, another pastor, Pastor John, prophesied, "The Lord wants you to stop trying to figure and just follow." Whoa! It's exactly what we needed to hear. Maybe it's what you need to hear as you read these words. Sometimes we want the end of the story first. But God could be asking you to stop trying to figure and just follow. One day at a time. One step at a time. Follow Him without having to have all of your questions answered. After all, that's what faith looks like. Faith is following when you don't have all of the answers, but trusting the One leading you.

When Jesus died a horrendous death on the cross, God was pleased with Him because He continued to trust His Father. I want to be like Jesus, trusting God even in death.

THE SCAM

I have story after story of the miracles of God in the lives of those

5 LEADING WITH JESUS

I love, in my life, and in our business. One in particular, I will never ever forget. My boys still mention it from time to time, because they remember what a devastating loss it truly was to our business. It wasn't as grand as the flood, but it still registered as a significant blow. Our wholesale business fell victim to a scam by a fake customer, "Sam Statler." We lost close to $14,000. Basically, a potential customer placed an order, and he gave us a credit card which we processed. When the money from the credit card cleared our bank, we processed a wire transfer to a supposed freight forwarder for the freight costs which is commonplace in our line of business as an importer. This practice is something we have done many times before without so much as a blink of an eye.

Several days after the wire transfer took place, the credit card companies began to call us to let us know the funds were being retrieved due to a possible fraud.

Possible fraud turned into, "Yes, it was fraud. And the money's gone."

We were sick about it. Our hearts were in our stomachs as several of us sat in a room with blank stares, tear filled eyes and dry throats. Is this real life? Did this really happen to us? We were being honest and doing our job like we always do? What now? And why in the world is this so hard? I asked God again, "Is this what you want us to be doing?" I'm certain I told him if it was, I needed Him to make it a little easier.

All any of us knew to do was to pray for restoration, peace, and wisdom. I reflected on Matthew 5:44, *"But I say to you, love your enemies and pray for those who persecute you."* We definitely felt persecuted. It wasn't necessarily our Christianity which was attacked, but it seemed like an attack of the enemy. However, I felt overwhelmed by the Holy Spirit to pray for Sam, the man behind the phone calls and emails. God didn't cause this to happen to us. We live in a fallen world with broken people. I feel like God allowed this

WHY IS IT SO HARD? 5

to happen, because He knows we are praying people, and He knew we would pray for those stealing from us. He knew we would pray for Sam. He knew we would continue to trust in His everlasting arms to hold us near. He knew those taking what was ours needed Him more than they needed the money in our bank account.

See, in business and in life, it's not always all about us and our growth. It's salient for us to be stretched while learning how to adapt to our circumstances. However, the picture is so much bigger than me and you. We prayed God would show Sam His love and His ways. We prayed for his soul. We prayed for direction for his life. We asked God to intervene and show His son, Jesus, to this man, this Sam. Not knowing if he would read it, we even sent him an email telling him how much Jesus loves him. If we truly want to be Jesus to the world, we have to be willing to pray for our enemies, just as the Bible instructs. *"You have heard that it was said, 'You shall love your neighbor and hate your enemy.' But I say to you, Love your enemies and pray for those who persecute you."* (Matthew 5:43) We have to pray for the one who steals from us whether it be an employee stealing time or a customer stealing our merchandise. Or in our case, a criminal taking $14,000 from our bank account we didn't have to lose.

I found myself praying several times over the next few weeks for Sam. My heart still breaks for people who don't know the love of my Father. I want to say to Sam, "If only you knew the provider of all, the one who loves you and will take care of you, the one who died for you, if only you knew Him the way I do then your life would be completely changed."

We found out that nothing could be done, in the natural, about our financial loss. The bank said the money was siphoned out of the account as soon as it was placed there. Sigh.

But you know what? We serve a supernatural God not bound or limited by the rules of earth. God is the only reason we are in business in the first place, and He doesn't need man's money to make

5 LEADING WITH JESUS

it work. There have been plenty of times over the years both of our businesses should have failed. Both remain open, but it's not by our own doings. We trusted God to return what was lost ten-fold, because He is a good God, and it's His very nature to return what is lost. Luke 6:38 says, *"Give, and it will be given to you. Good measure, pressed down, shaken together, running over, will be put into your lap. For with the measure you use it will be measured back to you."* We are givers, so we trusted God to come to our aid. We trust Him to remain true to His word. And when we pray, we remind Him of what His word says to us. In the Bible, Job survived terrible misfortune—far worse than what we had endured, and God worked it all out for Job's good, because Job loved the Lord with all of his heart. We believed God could do the same for us.

Most of all, we are trusting God heard our prayers of compassion for Sam, the responsible swindler. We know God loves Sam as much as He loves us. Sam is just a child of God's gone rogue. He represents a lot of crooked businessmen and women we see in the marketplace. But Jesus died on the cross for Sam, and he deserves the same grace and mercy we have received. One of the most wonderful things about God is His ability to redeem any person, even Sam. I have seen Him do it time and time again. I have experienced Him redeeming me.

Even after losing the $14,000, all I could say was, "God is good." My words may have sounded more like a low grumbling than a declaration from the hilltops, but I meant them all the same. I know He fights on our behalf. His love for us is deep and wide. He hurts when we hurt. We placed it all in His hands knowing He would work it out. It's during the trials of this life, God can shine. It's during the hard times when we don't know which decision is the right decision to make, He is able to pull us close to his chest and assure us of a future filled with hope. It's during times of despair, God can sharpen us and shape us making us more like Him. When Satan hands us evil schemes, God can turn it around giving us blessings and favor. The enemy goes around like a roaring lion seeking whom he may devour, but He can't have us. And during this ordeal, we decided he couldn't have our business.

GOD RETURNS WHAT IS LOST

A few months later God sent us a customer, out of the blue, who placed a large order with our company which financially redeemed what was lost. In the words of my husband, "One man stole from us, and God sent one man to redeem us." He actually spent more with us than what we originally lost. He even told my husband, without knowing our situation, he thought their paths had crossed for a reason. That's how God works. His very nature is that of a restorer.

Sometimes things are returned in unexpected ways. Sometimes the return can take a while to see. Sometimes the return is in our heavenly home and not while we are in our earthly homes. There seems to be a common myth in society which tells us, "If you get through this, everything will be okay." I am here to tell you that you are usually approaching a valley, in the valley, or coming out of the valley. Life is a cycle of mountaintops and valleys. You have to take the highs with the lows. There's not a time, this side of heaven, where you are going to be living in a perfect harmonious bliss – no matter the company, job title or personnel.

During the hard times when you are asking God the question, "Why is it so hard if I am in the middle of your will?" You can get into a trust versus hustle tug of war. When the money was originally taken, I started brainstorming ways to get it back. I'm a problem solver by nature. I am sure a lot of you reading this know exactly what I am talking about. I wanted to fix it. I know I have to work for what I want and need. But I felt like I was already doing all I could as a wife, mother, and full-time business owner.

5 LEADING WITH JESUS

Remember the story of Abraham, Sarah, and Hagar. Sarah got tired of waiting on her promise of a son so she urged Abraham to sleep with Hagar, the maidservant, who did become pregnant with a son, Ishmael. Sarah was hustling, not trusting. And it changed the course of history in a negative way. God did fulfill His promise to Abraham and Sarah, and Sarah gave birth to Isaac. Sarah's decision to hustle instead of trust caused division and warring which still continues today in the middle-east.

How many battles do you fight in your everyday life, because you don't allow God to fight for you? How many battles do you fight because you falsely feel like you are in control? Gradually, I am learning if I do all I can, God will take care of the rest. Even on days I could have possibly done more, He can fill in the gaps with His grace and mercy. The beautiful thing about grace is that it is always there when we need it. We can miss the mark in parenting, but God can fill in the gaps. We can handle a situation wrong, but God places his grace over it, like a soothing balm, and it all works out. He works it all out for our good when we love Him. (Romans 8:28)

You must remember our God is the God of more than enough. He shows up and says, "I've got this," during times of distress and pain. Life is not perfect. Things don't always make sense. Bad things happen to good people. But I have gotten to the point when I am delivered undesirable news, my eyes light up, and I can say with faith, "It's going to be exciting to see how God works this one out," and "I wonder who all He will use in the process to bring glory to His kingdom?" I hope He uses me. I hope I can be a part of the working out, a part of the solution.

At times, I want Him to work it out immediately, but God is always on time. *"There is a time for everything, and a season for every activity under heaven."* Ecclesiastes 3:1. During difficult times, we are eager for the pain to subside, for things to get easier, for the hustle to stop, but God will never allow us to walk through something meaningless. He can offer much to us when we're in the valley. There's always an opportunity for a deeper love, a deeper relationship with Him and with others, or an opportunity to learn to trust. When we find ourselves in the valley, we will experience some human emotions, but we can't set up camp in those valleys. We have to keep climbing the mountain.

In 2 Samuel, we read about David's third son Absalom. David's first two sons were dead, leaving Absalom as the rightful heir. Absalom was described as the best looking man in Israel. *"Now in all Israel there was no one who was praised as much as Absalom. From the sole of his foot to the crown of his head there was no blemish in him."* (2 Samuel 14:25) Absalom liked the attention, and he began to use it for his advantage. He started standing at the city gates and acting as king before it was time. *"So Absalom stole the hearts of the men in Israel."* (2 Samuel 15:6) It was not time for Absalom to be king, but he rushed his season. Rushing his season ultimately led to his death.

God never promised you your journey would be easy. But He did promise to be with you during the walk to your eternal home. (Hebrews 13:5) Unlike Absalom, you have to be patient while trusting God and His guidance or you could experience unwanted consequences. Don't rush your season and end up burned out. When you start to force your plan and your vision over God's, I believe it is harder for Him to bless your mess. I know He is able, and He will come to our rescue, but not without us feeling the negative effects. There are always consequences to our actions even when God keeps us from completely sinking.

BIKE RIDES, DIRTY FENCES, AND FIREWORKS

I get a vision of myself riding a bicycle as a little girl with my Daddy holding on to the seat to keep me upright. I am pedaling with all my

5 LEADING WITH JESUS

might and doing what I can to stay upright as I learn how to ride, but my Daddy's hand is there, on the seat, making sure I don't fall over. He's right beside me, balancing me, cheering me on. My Daddy never let go prematurely, and neither will my Heavenly Father.

If you want to get to where you're going, you are going to have to do some pedaling on the bike. You have to do your part, but you also have to trust God to keep you from falling. You have to trust Him to hold you up when you are weary, weak, and tired. When you wonder why it's so hard, you have to keep pedaling. You have to trust Him to hold tight to the seat of your bike. You will ride farther with Him than without Him. Most importantly, there will be times you need to sit in the sidecar and let God do the pedaling, trusting Him to lead and get you to where you're going. Oftentimes we think it's us getting us there, but it's always Him. During your "Why is this so hard?" moments, you can be more prone to make emotional decisions. I've always read if you want to maintain some level of fitness, you should never go to the grocery store hungry. Why? Because you will make an emotional decision based on your hunger and buy everything in sight based on your hunger. The same goes for making any major decisions; you have to separate your emotions from the problem.

One hot summer day, my thirteen-year-old son, Isaiah, agreed to pressure wash our fence for twenty dollars. He was desperate to earn some spending money; therefore, he was willing to do whatever it took to earn the money. David cranked up the pressure washer and showed him how to use it. He explained to him our fence had four sides, and he needed to make sure he was hitting all the sides. I saw Isaiah from the kitchen window working away, sweat pouring off his brow, cheeks red. I thought to myself, "It's good for him to learn how to work. I'm proud of his efforts." After he had finished spraying half the fence, he needed some help moving the pressure washer to a new location so he could reach the other half of the fence. As I went outside to see if I could assist him, I noticed there was still a faint

WHY IS IT SO HARD? 5

green layer of moss on most of the fence in which he had just slaved over to clean.

I inspected it, "Son, the fence is still dirty. I think you are going to have to go back over it." You would have thought I had just told him he wasn't going to get to play video games for the rest of his life. He had worked so hard, but his efforts hadn't paid off. It didn't make sense to him. "But I did everything you asked me to do!" His Dad offered to show him what he needed to do to correct his error. In an emotional outburst, he said, "You know what? I quit. I'm not doing it anymore. Forget it." He had forgotten his "WHY." In this case, it was because we, his parents, had told him to finish the task. It can be that simple. We do some things, because it's the right thing to do or God has told us to do them. Obviously, his attitude didn't fly at the Smith home, so we had to have a somewhat heated discussion with him about his attitude but also about making emotional decisions. While correcting him, I thought of my own desperate situations while working where I felt like I had done all I could do, but it wasn't enough. Thoughts of quitting are a normal but not acceptable part of being a human being. I don't know anyone who hasn't thought about giving up on their God dream. There are people I know who have given in to their emotions and quit the race too soon.

When you feel like you're sinking be reminded of *"Eye has not seen, nor ear heard, Nor have entered into the heart of a man the things which God has prepared for those who love Him."* 1 Corinthians 2:9 He has such good things in store for you. Things you can't begin to fathom. And Satan wants you to forfeit God's plan. He wants to thwart any efforts you attempt to advance the kingdom of heaven here on earth. You must stay focused and live a life expecting Him to deliver on His promises. His faithfulness in reminding us of His promises amazes me.

One summer, David urged me to take a girl's trip with one of my best friends. He knows the beach is one of my favorite places to be.

5 LEADING WITH JESUS

He has learned if I retreat to the sand and salt for a few days, I am like a new woman. He's a smart man. My friend and I loaded up my car and headed south. We made the most of our first day slathered in sunscreen soaking up the rays and listening to the ocean waves. That night, we ventured out for dinner followed by a stroll on the beach back to our hotel. We decided to sit in the sand, talk, and watch the water lap against the shore. The night seemed perfect except for a few harmless clouds delicately floating overhead. During the middle of our conversation and without warning, the first firework of many jetted off the end of a nearby pier exploding into the night sky. The fireworks looked like huge dandelions in the sky leaving the smoke residue to linger. I felt beckoned to make a wish, but not in a mystical or superstitious way. I never expected this beautiful display of lights and fire. I felt the Holy Spirit speak to me saying, "I have more in store for you than you can expect or imagine. Trust me." The night was perfect. When He writes your story, He pays attention to every little detail. He doesn't miss a thing, and He can speak to us when we least expect to hear from Him when we keep our spiritual ears open.

He's got me. He's got you. He's got us.

EXERCISE

1. What situation are you walking through that seems hard? Have you given it to the Lord? Letting go can be incredibly difficult, but make a decision every day to give it to the Lord. Through prayer tell Him, "Lord, this is bigger than me. I give it to you to work out. I know you will take care of me. I trust you. And I love you."

2. In what areas does your character need developing? Maybe you are impatient or easily offended or angered. It could be you struggle with control and trust. Do you see God's hand working in those areas of your life through your trials?

3. What are you expecting God to do in your life, your work, your family, your ministry?

4. Who has offended you or hurt you, but instead of clinging to the pain, you need to pray for them and release them to the Lord?

Chapter Six

CREATED WITH PURPOSE

    I love personality assessments so much that I give an abbreviated version of the Myers-Briggs Type Inventory (MBTI), created by Katharine Cook Briggs and her daughter Isabel Briggs Myers, to all prospective members of my team. A lot of good personality assessments are on the market, but I know the most about the MBTI so it's my tool of choice. The mother daughter duo created the assessment based on theories and teachings from Carl Gustav Jung. The MBTI measures personality types by determining the preferences of those who take it.

    When I started working with the assessment, Melissa, my supervisor at the time, explained it this way, "Take your pen and use your dominant hand to write your name on a piece of paper. Using your dominant hand feels natural. You have more control. It's the hand you prefer to use. Now, take your opposite, non-dominant hand, and write your name on your paper. How did that feel? Was it more difficult? Did it feel weird? Is your name even legible? You probably didn't prefer to use that hand, did you?" This example has always stuck with me. I am right handed, so of course my name looked better when written with my preferred hand, but I could still write my name

6 LEADING WITH JESUS

with my left hand. It was just uncomfortable and took more effort. This same example holds true for the various traits within your personality. You are capable of behaving outside your preferences, but it takes more effort. The same is true for those on your team.

I don't necessarily make hiring decisions based on MBTI results, but it does help me learn how people will react to stress, what inspires and energizes them, how organized they are, and if they are more visionary or action-oriented. The test gives varying degrees of each specific trait measured, and enables you to identify these traits in others so that you can find common ground, understand one another better, and build more productive and rewarding relationships.

When candidates show up for interviews, we give them an iPad explaining that we have a short assessment for them to take in order to learn more about their personality and what jobs we have that will fit them best. I tell them that the results help us to see which positions might be best suited for them within our company.

I believe the Lord instilled your personality and temperament into you from the moment you were conceived. I do not believe you were born a blank slate. While your upbringing can have an effect on your personality, it is your inborn traits that make you who you are. They give you your uniqueness, and they play a role in your destiny and purpose. For example, my oldest son cried a lot when he was a baby. We tried swaddling him and holding him close to comfort him. It only seemed to make his crying worse. Finally, I realized he just wanted to be left alone. He is now thirteen and still can't stand enclosed places or to be held down. He's a free-spirited adventure seeker. When my youngest son was born, he loved to be cuddled and rocked. It soothed him every time. He is now nine, and he still loves to cuddle and has a high need for physical touch. These are two very simple examples, but I'm sure you can pinpoint preferences you have had since childhood. Our teammates come to us with personality preferences and temperaments, as well. It's so easy to misunderstand someone because you process information differently from them. Unfortunately, the devil loves to use our differences against us to create division. However, the sooner you can recognize his tactics, the sooner you and your team can walk in unity.

A word of warning: personality assessments should never be used as a be-all and end-all solution, but they can be used as a tool (among many) that you use to understand people and how they process the world. The MBTI is exceptionally detailed, and if you are interested in learning more about it, I highly recommend pursuing online resources, as well as books that cover personality types. For our purposes in this chapter, I will cover a few of the basic principles the MBTI employs that I have found useful.

In the MBTI, each individual's personality is made up of four letters or possibilities: (E)xtraversion or (I)ntroversion; I(N)tuition or (S)ensing; (F)eeling or (T)hinking; and (J)udging or (P)rospecting. The first trait the MBTI measures is extraversion (E) versus introversion (I). People who are extremely extroverted can vary between never needing much time alone to needing a lot of alone time. There's also a population of people who are considered Ambiverts, who aren't extremely extraverted or introverted. I find myself in the Ambivert category. Extroverts generally get energy from being around other people. They are fueled by interacting with others and thrive in environments involving a lot of conversations. In fact, an extrovert can fall into depression and be unhappy if placed in a position which separates him or her from others. If they have to stay home for several days, they begin to feel off and out of sorts. Introverts typically draw energy from inside. This doesn't mean an introvert can't work with others or that he or she can't serve the public, but it means this person will have to take time to be alone and recharge. My youngest son, Spencer, is an introvert, and he describes people as "sucking the life from his battery." A lot of introverts can be fabulous when working with other people, but at the end of a busy day filled with numerous interactions, the introvert will probably feel drained. Spencer can talk the ears off of anyone who will listen if he has gotten to know the person well and feels safe. But after a long period of conversation, he will retreat to his room and play alone.

When an applicant applies for a job, I take a look at the degree of extraversion and introversion to decide which position will work best. I have noticed that when I hire an introvert during a busy season, I will find him or her finding tasks to perform that do not include dealing with customers. Thus, it works best to hire more extroverted individuals for customer service and sales roles. Introverted people typically enjoy working in our warehouse, where there are little to no interactions with the public.

It's important for you to know if your team members get energy from others or not. In my example above, if I hire an introvert, I know that when I find them off in a corner stocking shelves and avoiding customer interactions, they are likely just recharging their emotional batteries. Sometimes allowing them this time to regroup as they perform other tasks helps the rest of the day go more smoothly and results in greater productivity and job satisfaction.

The second two traits measured by the Myers-Briggs Type Indicator are Sensing (S) and Intuition (N). In a nutshell, intuitive individuals like to come up with big ideas and enjoy looking into the future. They process information in a more abstract way. Conversely, sensing individuals like to take in information through their five senses, put action to ideas, and make things happen. You need both types of people on your team. I have found that it's good to have a mix of sensing and intuitive individuals for the kind of work we do. As you learn more about each type, you will find what works best for you and your organization. Personally, I find myself on the intuitive side of the spectrum, but I am not an extreme case. I'm a get it done kind of girl and like to see results and not just dream up ideas.

The third set of traits, Thinking (T) and Feeling (F), are critically important when it comes to conflict management and how you talk to your team members. Given the names, it's tempting to assume that a thinker is simply someone who gives decisions more thought, and a feeler bases decisions on emotions, but that's not the case. Thinkers are individuals who first consider logic when making decisions, while a feeler's primary concern when making decisions are the people involved. Thinkers are typically blunt and to the point when speaking to others. He or she may not consider how the person on the receiving end of a statement will feel at the end of the conversation. This doesn't mean feelers don't think logically, but a feeler is more concerned with the relationships involved in a decision than a thinker may be. Oftentimes, thinkers can hurt the feelings of feelers without even knowing it. On the other hand, feelers will typically spend a lot of time thinking about how a comment or decision is going to make a person feel before saying whatever is on his or her mind. For example, a thinker might say, "The logical thing to do is xyz," while the feeler will say, "We need to think about how this decision will impact everyone involved." Neither approach to decision-making is right or wrong. In fact, I have found that arriving at the best decision requires the involvement of both thinkers and feelers. In our business, I am a feeler, and David is more of a thinker. Together, we can usually come up with a solution that is both logical and emotionally considerate of those around us. If you lean one way or another, I would suggest finding someone on your team to bounce your ideas off of so you can find a balanced approach to decision making.

The final two traits covered by the MBTI are Judging (J) and Prospecting (P). Judging doesn't mean someone is criticizing your every move and making hasty assumptions about you. Judging individuals tend to like to have a plan A, B and C. They like to make decisions, stick to them, and move along with their day. Typically, they have an idea of how much time it will take to accomplish a task. Most extreme judging types, like myself, can tell you what time it is at any point in the day without the help of a clock. They love a good plan and usually live by a calendar. Prospecters are your go-with-the-flow individuals. They prefer to keep options open and can sometimes drive their counterparts, the Judgers, crazy. Prospecters are usually late for most appointments or are sliding in at the last minute, while Judgers arrive early and well-prepared. A good plan calms my anxiety and helps me feel less chaotic. David is a Prospecter. He's not a fan of concrete plans, and he never knows what time it is. Many times he thinks it's been ten minutes, and it's been two hours. It can be frustrating, but when you learn the traits of those you work with, you are able to show them a little more grace and mercy without writing them off as disrespectful or rude. It's important to be able to determine the difference between a personality difference and a character flaw. Missed deadlines don't bother the Prospecting type as much. In the grand scheme, it is important for the Judging type to learn to bend and flex and for the Prospecting type to learn structure and follow through. It's all about finding a balance and personal growth. God knew when he created us that the world would need all types. I am glad we aren't all the same. Aren't you?

Our team discusses our types and looks to the assessment as a way to learn inside information about one another. If you give a personality assessment to a new employee, it's important to take a moment to let them know where you found the assessment and inform them of where more information can be found about the various types. People love to learn information about themselves, and whether you hire them or not, you will be doing them a favor by helping them gain more insight into their preferences.

LEARN YOUR PERSONALITY STYLE

It's important for you, as a leader, to learn your personality style, and how to bend and flex to do what's needed for success. Share your type with your team so you aren't potentially misunderstood. Your personality type should never be used as an excuse or a crutch, but should be used as a way to identify your strengths and weaknesses, and understand the differences between your personality and others. If you visit www.16personalities.com, you will find a free test that you and your teammates can take, as well as detailed descriptions of each type. You will also get helpful information on how to manage the different personality types. Be sure to take into consideration that each individual is an expert on his or herself. If you choose to assess your team, consider a team meeting where you talk about the results and see who on your team scored similarly versus those who seem to be polar opposites. Take a look at your Thinkers and Feelers and discuss whether any of the Feelers have gotten their feelings hurt by a Thinker. Some of the strengths and weaknesses listed online may not be correct based on where a person is in the journey of life. Hopefully, as time passes, people grow and develop skills for overcoming weaknesses and blind spots. Despite results, I think it's good for all personality types to seek a balance between the letters, because ultimately, we want to make sure we are honoring the Lord with our actions and our personalities.

EXERCISE

1. Go to www.16personalities.com and take the Free Personality Assessment. What are your results?

2. Based on the results, what are your strengths? Do you agree?

3. Based on the results, what are your weaknesses? Do you agree?

Chapter Seven

EXPECTATIONS, ACCOUNTABILITY AND CORRECTION

I have been let down so many times by the people around me. Whether it is an unfinished project or hearing about gossip in the workplace, it can be exhausting. I often have to remind myself that if I didn't allow my team members to hold me up, they couldn't let me down. So many times I have come home with physical aches and pains, because of the stress I was carrying. Stress I was not able to figure out how to give to God. Stress that stemmed from feeling like everything was my problem to solve, only I wasn't sure how. We hear people say "Leadership isn't for the faint of heart," and, boy, is that true. My heart has grown faint many times. I have unofficially turned in my two weeks notice to my husband more than once. In fact, it's embarrassing how many times I have threatened to quit in the last year.

Communicated expectations can be hard to meet, but they are easier to meet than expectations that are not communicated at all. Clear and concise job descriptions are a must for any position and do a good job of laying out expectations. This may seem like a no-brainer, but if your team members don't know what you expect, they won't live up to your expectations. Clear communication when new

7 LEADING WITH JESUS

projects are assigned or new job duties given, in verbal and written format, is a must. If there's any wriggle room, your team members will wriggle. So your first step toward setting achievable expectations is to make sure every responsibility is covered in a job description. It's easy to find free job description templates online to tweak and make your own. Not only are job descriptions a handy reference tool during performance evaluations; if you ever have a question about who is supposed to do what, you have a job description for reference. Don't let it surprise you if your team members test their limits to see if you will enforce the duties assigned.

COHESIVE LEADERSHIP

It's important your team members know who to take directions from regarding projects, and it's important that you don't have multiple people giving different instructions. There is nothing more frustrating than a team member being told one thing by one person and another thing by another person. It causes confusion, resentment and even anger. It also decreases productivity and causes division.

When I first joined the business, David and his dad would sometimes tell people to do varying things. They had different ways of completing the same tasks. It was driving the team members crazy. No one wanted to disrespect either of them, but they weren't sure what to do, which caused them to do nothing at times. It also caused them to come to me seeking clarity. I know first hand it is not fun to be caught in the middle. Both of these activities cost our business time and money, and it cost our team members their sanity. To stop the madness, it was important for us to set up parameters around who would assign which tasks, and who trumped the other person. There needs to be one single person in charge calling the final shot every time. Since my husband and I operate the business together, I decided to allow him to make the final decisions. It's not about me

EXPECTATIONS, ACCOUNTABILITY AND CORRECTION

giving up control, it's about me following God's advice to submit to my husband. Embarrassingly, I don't always submit without a fight, but I do yield to his leadership. David is submitted to the Lord; therefore I should submit to Him when he is working to do the right thing and follow God's lead. Thankfully, he listens to me and values my input and decision-making abilities. We have mutual respect for one another.

I know a lot of women in today's world get upset about having to submit to their husbands. Some have trouble with 1 Corinthians 14: 35 which says, *"And if they want to learn something, let them ask their own husbands at home; for it is shameful for women to speak in church."* Although this admonition can seem off-putting on the surface; when you dig into deeper communication with your spouse at home, it builds intimacy as the word is learned and studied together. Essentially, I believe Paul is instructing women and men to have intimate conversations with one another. I don't believe it is there to degrade or put women in their "place." God loves us, as women, and He wants what is best for us. Maybe you and your spouse don't lead together, but your unity in general life issues can make an impact on your success in your workplace.

Psalms 133:1 says, *"How good and pleasant it is when God's people live together in unity!"* I think we could even say, "How good and pleasant it is when God's people WORK together in unity!" A unified work place has a totally different vibe to it once you have felt the effects of a workplace running on poisonous attitudes, gossip and discord.

As a leader, it is up to you to work hard for unity. This means if you get the hint of something bad going down, you have to address it immediately. Letting it fester and spread like a bad infection will only make the problem worse. You can apply unity to any partnership. There have been times I knew Satan was out to destroy the unity my husband and I had. Sometimes, we can rub like sandpaper against

7 LEADING WITH JESUS

our partners. It's important to call Satan out on his schemes, and let him know you aren't falling for it. He is the enemy, not your partner.

When I "joined the crazy," as I lovingly call my first few days on the job, David and I had very different approaches to handling problems. I am a "let's do it today" kind of girl, and he is a "let's wait," kind of guy. There's a balance between those two which we have found. But sometimes, because of the nature and business of the job and how busy my day can get, I can't always handle things NOW, like I would like to. On the flip side, I have to realize when it is time to make room in my schedule and prioritize issues that threaten the unity and effectiveness of my team. Anything causing division becomes a priority.

MATTHEW 18 PRINCIPLE

One of the most important biblical principles we can follow when dealing with any kind of conflict in our lives is the Matthew 18 principle. This scriptural mandate tells us, *"If your brother sins against you, go and show him his fault, just between the two of you."* It's important to address conflict head on, in love, but with intentionality. It's important that the person with whom we have conflict, or whom a team member has conflict, is called into the conversation.

When issues arise, we have to be open to hearing all sides of the story. It's important to begin to teach our teammates to have open minds and hearts, as well. There's always two sides to every story. We can't have our minds made up before we go into a meeting with someone on how it is all going to play out. We also have to be open to the Holy Spirit and His voice. Sometimes He'll call you to be silent when you're ready to voice every opinion and objection you have to what someone is doing. Sometimes, team members can share information with us we didn't anticipate, changing our perspectives and the outcome of the meeting. I remember a particular team

EXPECTATIONS, ACCOUNTABILITY AND CORRECTION

member who never seemed to ask questions when given a project. After awhile, I began to conclude that maybe she was carrying a fear of asking questions over from a previous employer. I was right. Another team member was regularly paranoid people were talking about her behind her back. This had happened to her at a previous job, so she expected it to happen again. Just like any relationship, people can bring in their baggage. It's up to us, as leaders, to help them unpack the baggage, and find trust and support in their current culture.

If you go into a meeting with a closed mind, you will only hear what you want to hear, validating your own conclusions. But, on the flip side, you also have to use discernment and wisdom, asking God to help you to see the light in the darkness and to decipher the truth from lies. Before any type of possible conflict, it's important you are "prayed-up" before meeting with someone. Ask the Lord to reveal any ulterior motives. Ask Him to give you the words to speak. Ask Him to allow your supernatural ears to hear what you may not be hearing in the natural. If possible, open your meeting with prayer. I understand some job places may not be open to this practice, but if you are able, it's amazing what happens when you pray with someone before a difficult conversation. It can be even more beneficial to pray with them after the meeting to promote unity and understanding.

FORGIVE BUT RECORD

It is also important to document, document, document every conversation. I know, you may be saying, "The Bible tells us to keep no records of wrong," (1 Corinthians 13:5) and I agree. We can't love people well and continuously hold their wrongdoings over their heads. However, from a human resources perspective, we have to keep good records on issues and concerns that arise with our team members.

We should also record the good our team members do.

7 LEADING WITH JESUS

Remember the Awesome Box? It's not fair to only judge employees' performances based on what they messed up or where they missed the mark. If we do so, it is impossible to conduct fair assessments.

Good record keeping helps you to see the big picture. Face it, leaders do a lot on any given day, and we aren't going to remember from week to week what someone is doing well. More than likely, we will remember what they are doing wrong. It seems to be human nature for our memories to hold more tightly to the negative. This is why 1 John 1:9 is so powerful, *"If we confess our sins he is faithful and just to forgive us our sins and cleanse us from all unrighteousness."* If God can forgive us, we should be able to forgive others.

I have tried to get into the habit whenever I notice an employee doing something wrong of first asking, "What did she do well this week?" Employees are flesh and blood people who make mistakes. What's important is whether you have correctable or rebellious people. The correctable team member can be developed and helped along. The rebellious, manipulative person has to have a change of heart or his time with our organization won't last long. I've learned to spot manipulation more quickly than I used to. One sign of manipulation that is a huge red flag for me is the victim mentality. An employee trying to manipulate you will always be the victim; even if she takes responsibility for her actions, somehow she believes it really wasn't her fault. When you are trying to walk out your Christian faith in the marketplace, she will attempt to use it against you with comments like, "Some Christian you are." Or when you have to let her go for a policy violation, she'll respond with, "After all I did for you?!" Guilt will be doled out, causing you to feel like you are the one who did something wrong by following company policy. Typically, these employees will suck your emotions dry. You will find yourself spending loads of time dealing with the drama left in their wake, or trying to help them have a better life; however, your advice will fall on deaf ears as they continue to make poor life decisions. Most of the time emotional manipulators know what to say, when to say it, and who will play their game. In our business, my husband's partnership is invaluable to me. He doesn't play the game, nor does he get as emotionally attached to our teammates. He cares for them, but they know early on he won't play their game. It's important to know yourself and your weaknesses so you don't fall victim to lies and manipulation. If you do have a tender heart or the spiritual gift of mercy, recognize it, and have someone on your team who can help redirect you when you begin to question your decisions and sanity. No matter the type of employee, it's important to say what you mean and mean what you say, but it's especially true of an emotional manipulator. If you don't, all the boundaries will be pushed and eventually crossed.

We also have to remember, as leaders, we are often in the role of growing our organizations and companies. Sometimes, that entails being able to make or protect profits. Our profits shouldn't be at the expense of treating people poorly. However, there are times we must minimize our liabilities to protect the livelihood of our companies and organizations. We owe our employees a safe work environment, but allowing an employee to stick around who is no longer doing the work or who is causing turmoil in the organization can be likened to running a charity.

REBELLION

The rebellious employee is going to push the limits, try to bend the rules, whisper lies, divide your team, practice manipulation, and ultimately cause you pain. She will make you question your leadership, and your team members' confidence levels will suffer. You may begin to wonder if you really are as crazy as you once thought. This employee will do the least amount of work as possible and can usually be found barking orders to other teammates instead of leading

7 LEADING WITH JESUS

by example. It's also possible that this person could be a workhorse, accomplishing much during the day, including causing division amongst your team. Or maybe this employee meets all the deadlines and completes all job duties, but he has a deep character issue which you can't fix. In some cases, these employees have not accepted Jesus as Lord of their life, and they are not living to the standards He raises. Or maybe the person has accepted Jesus, but he is not allowing him to reign over every part of his life. It could be due to a lack of maturity or a mental illness.

Jesus led by example, and as a business leader aiming to be Jesus in the marketplace, we have to lead by example, too. He didn't put up with nonsense and lies. He called people out when they were in the wrong, and He asked thought-provoking questions to get His point across. He also encouraged people to seek help when necessary.

THE STORY OF RUTH AND NAOMI

Let's take a look at the wedding story from Cana of Galilee referenced in John 2:1-12. Jesus's mother came to him to inform him there was no more wine. Jesus rebuked her when she asked saying, *"Woman, what does this have to do with you and me?"* Basically, "This is my work and my responsibility. I've got it under control. It's not something we must work out together." He had authority over her and he claimed it.

As much as I value input and teamwork, there's a fine line between your employees managing you and you managing them. Some situations aren't their burdens to bear. We have to be confident and honest with team members who question our authority. It's imperative for employees to know you have a job to do and they have a job to do. Together, you'll be able to accomplish company goals.

EXPECTATIONS, ACCOUNTABILITY AND CORRECTION

If you feel a team member is undermining your authority and going against the grain, pray and ask God to reveal anything in your heart you could be projecting onto the person or situation. Seek to find any insecurities you may have as a leader that you are carrying into the conversation. Ask God for guidance as He leads your actions and gives you the right words to say to the person. Ask Him to be honored and glorified in your words. Ask Him for teachable moments and opportunities. Never go into the conversation angry. You can be firm, bold and direct, but your anger should be dealt with before the team member is approached. Make notes before talking to the associate so you can stay on track. Remember you are representing Jesus in these talks. This doesn't mean you are a doormat and have to coddle the person. It does mean you should execute discipline in love —and that can be hard. Unless you have shown the person how much they mean to you leading up to this point, it will be even harder.

HIRE WELL

Some say you won't have many issues with your team members if you hire the right people from the beginning, and in a perfect world, we always hire the right people. However, it's not a perfect world, and some people are really good at nailing a job interview. Once that person gets the job, he or she can act like a different person from the one you interviewed. Or they may not actually have the skill set needed for the job. And let's face it, sometimes the pool from which you selected an employee are not full of the best candidates. You probably hired the best you could hire at the time. We have hired employees, who had a "fake it until you make it" attitude. We trusted them on the front-end and didn't require a demonstration of skills. We lacked wisdom in those moments. To avoid doing the same, do your due diligence; hire slowly, interview multiple times and check references. Most of all, pray for God to send you the people you

7 LEADING WITH JESUS

need. He is faithful to hear our cries for help. There will be times God sends you people who need you more than you need them. You will have something to offer during a season, and God has you on an assignment to give it away. Be open to accepting these assignments from Him. Admit you don't always make the right decisions, but be sure to make prayerful ones. At the end of the day, you may not understand why the person was a part of your organization, but you can trust God had a purpose for them for a season.

DIFFICULT CONVERSATIONS

Difficult conversations are the least favorite aspect of my job. In fact, when I surveyed my team, it was unanimous amongst my managers. No one liked to deal with difficult employees or customers. I'm guessing you don't like these conversations either. I have never seen someone super excited about having to reprimand an employee or tell a customer he can't have his way. But these conversations help us to grow. Personally, they help me to realize my capacity for loving others and the kind of love God has for me. Each time we bring someone in for disciplinary reasons, they are usually nervous. Sometimes they jokingly equate it to being called into the principal's office at school. Even though, at times, I call them in to share the good news, it can still be a scary place. In the days and hours leading up to a difficult conversation, I have experienced an upset stomach, lack of sleep, and been a little more on edge than normal. Maybe you can relate to these feelings. I don't know anyone who loves conflict, but conflict is necessary for growth in any relationship. Before having a tough conversation, I ask myself:

1. Did this person know what was expected? Did I or another team member communicate clearly? Is this a normal pattern of behavior for him or her, or is there something more going on?

EXPECTATIONS, ACCOUNTABILITY AND CORRECTION

2. Does this person know there are consequences to their actions? If so, do they know the repercussions for their actions?

3. What action will be taken to make sure change takes place? What is fair?

It's always important to be prepared for these types of conversations — prepared, but flexible. You may have to change your tactics once you have talked to the team member. People don't always realize what they are doing wrong, or they don't realize the problems it is causing you, your business or your team. Preparation gives you the chance to open the doors of communication and explain your position more clearly, letting the person know the consequences of future misbehavior(s). It also allows you to set up a corrective action plan to help the person succeed. Lastly, always document corrective conversations for clarity and accountability purposes. It's important to discipline team members who are not meeting clearly defined expectations, or who are bickering and disrupting morale because of toxic attitudes, such as jealousy and negativity. In our workplace, we have steps we follow when handling discipline issues. First, we talk to the person in an informal way making sure he/she knows the rules. If the behavior continues, we call the person in for a more formal sit-down. This can include a detailed discussion or a corrective action plan if we feel it warrants immediate action. The severity of the offense directs our next steps. If a corrective action plan (a written agreement between employer and employee) is in place, we give the team member x number of days to correct documented behavior. If the behavior is not corrected, the team member is either written up or terminated. Sometimes we write the employee up and send him/her home for several days to reflect and decide if our place of employment is the right place for him/her. When we look at examples in the Bible, Jesus was fairly direct when

7 LEADING WITH JESUS

it came to discipline. He was also brutally honest. Jesus corrected Peter's jealousy of John by telling him, *"If it is my will that he remain until I come, what is that to you? You follow me!"* (John 21:22). He was basically telling Peter not to worry about what someone else was doing and to only worry about what he was supposed to be doing. If you've been in leadership long, you have probably already encountered jealousy in the workplace. It's a mean and ugly beast, leading employees down a dangerous road of comparison and disappointment. In fact, it can be one of the main reasons your team is in discord. One team member is watching another team member and how you interact. Comparing begins and ends with disparaging thoughts and motives.

I like the analogy of water and oxygen as a metaphor for discussing how both are very different, just like our employees, but both have their rightful place in our lives and places of work . Both water and oxygen are necessary for human survival. Water can be felt, tasted and seen. Its vastness can't be missed when we look at lakes, rivers and oceans. It's easy to notice when water dries up or is no longer where it once was. Oxygen, an equally important survival agent, is typically unseen. We don't know we don't have any until we can't breathe...like when we slide into our spanx on Sunday mornings. Explaining an employee's value can be very beneficial. Most employees living in a healthy spiritual place won't suffer as much with jealousy as those who are not living the life God intended them to live. Why? Because those guys and gals aren't finding their value and worth in the Father who created them. They are finding their value in applause, recognition and job titles. In addition, the negative voices and disappointing nods of those around them lead them to experience deep insecurities and broken places too painful to touch. When in graduate school for my counseling degree, we were taught, "Hurt people, hurt people." The human need for approval, acceptance and praise can lead to comparison and jealousy. It's not only found in our

EXPECTATIONS, ACCOUNTABILITY AND CORRECTION

employees, though, it can be found in anyone we lead; from small group members and our children; to our church family, and, gulp, even ourselves.

YOU'RE NOT THE SAVIOR

Remember, even though you are Jesus in the marketplace, you can't save people. There will be people outside of your reach. You will give them chance after chance after chance, and they will continue to take advantage of you and their team members. There will be team members in desperate situations causing you to want to rescue them, but you can't. You're not Jesus. John 15 tells us that Jesus is the vine and we are the branches. We have to abide in Him. Our employees have to abide in Him, not in us. We are not their superheroes or savior. If we aren't careful, we can find ourselves feeling responsible for their decisions, but we aren't.

Yes, we want to give people a good place to work, and we want to be great leaders, but we can't take responsibility for every aspect of their lives. We want to show them grace and mercy, but if we don't hold them accountable, we aren't loving them well.

Part of loving people well involves reprimanding them in private as much as possible. Recently, I was at a fast food restaurant when a young girl behind the cash register got my order wrong. When she told her manager what had happened, her manager began to correct her in a loud voice to the point I felt terribly uncomfortable. The manager was talking to the girl in a frustrated and angry tone as she told her that she should be learning her register and spending more time going through each screen as opposed to doing other tasks. I have felt that same kind of anger toward an employee rise up inside of me like a volcano ready to explode, damaging all in its wake. That's why it's so important to control our emotions. The cashier's head hung low in defeat, and our eyes never met again during my visit. I know

7 LEADING WITH JESUS

she was humiliated. I was humiliated for her. The person preparing the food in the back saw what happened and mouthed, "I'm sorry," to me. She felt uncomfortable, too. I wanted to reassure the girl it was okay and encourage her, but I felt it best to slip out quietly with my egg and biscuit.

You can't control your team members' emotions or how they feel about you or others on your team, but you can control your emotions and reactions. You can't force your team members out of their abusive relationship or make them go to church. You can't solve all of their financial issues or figure out who will watch their children when you make the schedule out for the week. You can't anticipate their every need, and to be expected to anticipate the needs of a capable human is completely unfair. Just as they are humans, you are human, too. You have limitations and can't solve every problem chucked at you. There will be days you feel you have been treated like a robot. Sometimes it's hard for team members to see management as people, too. Some seem to think our feelings can't be hurt, or that we don't feel the sting of them not asking us to be in the group photo at the company Christmas party. It's in these moments your identity has to be so rooted in Jesus, the Vine. You have to know who you are and whose you are. You have to remember you've been set apart. You are different, because God has placed you in a different position. You aren't above them, but you serve them as their leader. Just as Jesus was treated differently by those in the world, we can expect the same when we bear the name of Christ, regardless of our position.

The Bible teaches in John 15:18-21, *"If the world hates you, know that it has hated me before it hated you. If you were of the world, the world would love you as its own; but because you are not of the world, but I chose you out of the world, therefore the world hates you. Remember the word that I said to you: 'A servant is not greater than his master.' If they persecuted me, they will also persecute you. If they kept my word, they will also keep yours. But all these things they will*

EXPECTATIONS, ACCOUNTABILITY AND CORRECTION 7

do to you on account of my name, because they do not know him who sent me."

Anytime you face controversy in the workplace, you have to remember you aren't always going to be liked or loved. Remember Jesus, the perfect man, was persecuted. When living for Jesus, persecution is to be expected. If you aren't experiencing any persecution, you probably aren't doing something right. Think about the apostle Paul and all of the time he spent in a nasty prison before being beheaded due to his drive to advance the Kingdom. I'm sure he had to focus on the "Why" many times to make it through each day. I can't imagine knowing I was about to have my head chopped off. It makes the trials I have faced pale in comparison.

Think back to your WHY. If you choose to honor Jesus in your life, whatever your job, you are going to be attacked and persecuted by the enemy. The enemy will use willing people to accomplish his mission. When the hard knocks come, and you wonder what you did to deserve such harsh treatment by either an employee or a customer, you must remind yourself that the enemy is out to destroy your vision, culture and identity.

THE LORD FIGHTS FOR YOU

What happens when we face a situation where we have been wronged? What if we have a rightful lawsuit regarding our business? What if we know we would even win the lawsuit? We have found ourselves in that very position a few times over the course of the years. We were encouraged by numerous people to sue over a multitude of things. Paul instructed the Corinthians not to go to court against one another (1 Corinthians 6:1-8) Granted, Paul was mainly addressing the church and instructing church members not to take other church members to court, but still, what kind of example is it to the world if we live just like them being sue-happy and taking our

7 LEADING WITH JESUS

grievances to the courts instead of to the King? Imagine the testimony we can live out by separating ourselves from the world. We have to trust Exodus 14:14, *"The Lord will fight for you, and you have only to be silent."* If a court dispute can be avoided, it should be. However, there will be times a lawsuit is the only way to recoup damages that threaten the livelihood of your business. There will be times where people around you must be held accountable and take responsibility for what belongs to them.

In the case of our flood, city officials had told us for years the pumps and drainage system in our area was on the list to be upgraded. Having a mortgage on our building meant we were in it for the long haul. Every time we would hear the news of repairs and upgrades, our hopes soared. Year after year, our parking lot would fill up with water, and someone from our place of business would have to call or visit the city to let them know the pumps weren't working effectively. We reported how the drainage ditches were full of garbage making it difficult for water to drain. Our parking lot would fill with water to the point of people having to move their vehicles to higher ground. Once, a grant was received. Our business was told that it was included in the location of places to repair. We were given several dates which came and passed. And then imagine our distress when we were told the grant money had all been spent on another area and no repairs were in sight for us. We recognize the city in which we call home to our business is not one of wealth and resources, but we do expect them to do what we were told for years and years that they were going to do in an effort to protect us and the people in the neighborhood behind us from heavy rain. At some point along the way, most city officials decided it best not to communicate with us any longer. When communication ceased, we felt we had no choice but to hire an attorney to act on our behalf in order to get answers and to press for repairs to be made to the drainage system and the pumps. Our goal is still not to sue the city, but to ensure the pumps and

EXPECTATIONS, ACCOUNTABILITY AND CORRECTION

drainage system are running as best as possible so we can minimize the chances of our building and the neighborhood flooding again. During the last round of heavy rain in our area, we were told the pumps were set to turn on sooner and the drainage system had been cleaned out. Praise God for progress.

DON'T BUY THE LIES

Friends, leadership can mess with your mind. The enemy will use it as a playground if you have any doubts and insecurities about your abilities or where God has placed you. Satan will tell you people would be better off with a different leader or if you led a different way, an easier way, things would improve. He will tell you that you are incapable of leading. He will tell you to sue. He will encourage you to gossip about your team. He will make you question every decision you have made, and he will try to pit you against your partners and teammates. He will ask you, "Who do you think you are?" He will play mind games with you and make you paranoid thinking everyone is against you. He will tell you there is no way out and it is way past time for you to throw in the towel. He is the master of lies and deceit, so don't listen to him. In your weak moments, God will give you strength, just as He has given me strength. The first step is recognizing the enemy's voice is not God's voice. Learn to abide in the vine and listen to the right voice, your Father's voice. Doing so will change how you do life and business.

EXERCISE

1. Do you have an accountability plan with those you manage? Do they know what is expected of them?

2. Who holds you accountable?

7 LEADING WITH JESUS

3. Take time to create an organizational chart that you can refer to regarding who makes which decisions and who reports to whom. Make sure it is shared with your employees and displayed prominently in your organization, so there is no confusion.

4. How updated is your Policies and Procedures Manual? It should be reviewed annually for revisions. If you don't have one, you can find lots of great templates for free online to get you started. Possible topics to include: dress code, absences, cell phone usage, time-off requests, leave time, children and pets in the workplace, employee discounts, conflict resolution steps, and usage of company property and equipment.

5. What lies about your leadership style is Satan trying to convince you to believe? Learn to recognize God's voice over Satan's and only believe what God says about you.

Chapter Eight

DISCOVERING YOUR LEADERSHIP STYLE AND SETTING BOUNDARIES

If you google "leadership styles," you will get 354,000,000 search results along with this definition, "A leadership style refers to a leader's characteristic behaviors when directing, motiving, guiding, and managing groups of people. Great leaders can inspire political movements and social change. They can also motivate others to perform, create, and innovate."

It's really hard to separate who you are from your leadership style. Who you are will flow into your decisions and interactions with the people who work for you and with you. I remember a few times being hurt by people in the workplace, because I had allowed myself to get close to them. I considered them "friends." Most leadership seminars and books will tell you it's not good for you to be friends with those you manage. I agree it can be difficult to hire a friend and manage them, but it can be hard for a relational leader not to care for the people they are trying to supervise and mentor every day.

Several times out of hurt, I would say to my husband, "I am not getting close to anyone at work again. I just end up getting my feelings hurt and feeling violated." I usually distance myself for a few days, but before I know it, I am all-in with my people again. My leadership style is one centered around our employees being a family. Some of our team members jokingly call me "Momma." I want to be as professional as possible with my team, but I also recognize that we are all human and much more productive when we can let our hair down and have a little fun while getting our work done. I might tell a joke or use sarcasm to make a point with team members who respond well to those communication styles.

STANDING FIRM

I hadn't been working for the company long when I got my first nickname. A long-time employee, Matthew, and I were working quickly to make up memorial pieces for the upcoming decoration season, which is a southern tradition of decorating graves of loved ones. To prepare, we make up saddles, blankets, vase inserts, and tomb clips filled with artificial flowers. Lots of melted glue chips are used during the process. We melt our glue in large electric skillets. It's a pretty nice craft hack when you work with as much glue as we do on a daily basis. Customers can place custom orders for the flowers or they can purchase what we have on the shelves. One night, we were all working late. We had gotten a bit delirious when Matthew made a sarcastic comment to me. My quick reply was, "I will dip your face in that glue pan if you aren't careful." His eyes got big before he burst into laughter. Obviously, I wasn't serious, and this is not a comment I would make to just any employee, but I have known Matthew and his family for a long time. We actually grew up in the same small town in Tennessee. Matthew had never seen this side of me, so he began calling me, "Big Sandy." He calls this my alter ego. My nature is to be loving, kind and nurturing, but there are times that call for tough love, no nonsense and firmness. Having this nickname helps make leadership a little easier. Long-time employees will tell new employees about Big Sandy, and we all get a good laugh, but the point is conveyed that we have rules and standards in our place of business. We love people and expect accountability.

BE THE KIND OF LEADER YOU WOULD FOLLOW

We have to learn the personalities of each member of our team. The faster we can learn who they are and how they work, the faster we can have productive conversations. It's important to explain to new team members how you communicate and how you choose to lead. For example, we tell new members how we have done everything in the store, and we would never ask them to do something we aren't willing to do ourselves. They see us putting out stock, taking out the trash, and sweeping the floors. Ideally, leaders should be focused on leading, using the majority of their time for making decisions, casting and carrying out the vision, dealing with finances, etc. However, it is always good for morale for team members to see that you are not afraid to do what you are asking them to do. Isn't that exactly what Jesus did? He modeled how He wanted us to behave.

Boundaries have to be in place, but I don't think the development of personal relationships at work is a black and white issue. For example, I might talk to my team members about their personal lives if they bring it up to me first. I may offer godly advice and prayer if they ask what I think or if I feel the Holy Spirit prompting me to do so. How else can I share God's word with them if I refuse to engage in any personal conversations? Over the years, I have had several team members who have experienced marital issues. Haven't most of us had marriage issues, even if we have only been married a few days? It's a part of life. There have been many conversations I have had on the couch in my office with team members about how to walk through tough times with your spouse. I have encouraged them by sharing about the time when my marriage was on the rocks, mainly due to being overworked and weary. I tell them a little about why we found

8 LEADING WITH JESUS

ourselves in that space and how God repaired and restored us.

There have been mothers, who have asked me for advice regarding their teething baby or toddler, who is throwing tantrums. I have walked through those events with my two sons already, so I share with them my experiences. Titus 2:3-5 says, *"Likewise, teach the older women to be reverent in the way they live, not to be slanderers or addicted to much wine, but to teach what is good. Then they can urge the younger women to love their husbands and children, to be self-controlled and pure, to be busy at home, to be kind, and to be subject to their husbands, so that no one will malign the word of God."*

Some of you reading this may be saying, "But if I mention God in my workplace, I could be fired." I do realize that is a possibility, but that doesn't have to stop you from modeling Jesus-like behavior. One of our team members told another team member, "Before I ever talked to you, I knew you carried the peace of God. You didn't have to say a word." People are watching you. If we, as Christians, live and lead like the world tells us to live and lead, we aren't going to look like Jesus. We are going to look like the world. When we choose to stand out and lead like Jesus led, it will be noticed. People aren't attracted to us, they are attracted to the Jesus who lives inside of us.

BOUNDARIES

While you're leading, I hope you will set some boundaries. For example, just because you are trying to take care of people and mentor them, it doesn't mean you have to be available to them 24/7. In fact, it is unhealthy for you to do so. If you don't have the mental, physical or emotional energy to answer phone calls or texts after hours, don't. Even Jesus retreated during difficult times to spend some time alone. It's a theme throughout the gospels that is often overlooked. Every leader needs time alone. When Jesus spent time alone, he dealt with grief and meditated on decisions He needed to make. When we have the hustle and bustle of the world spinning in our thoughts, never unplugging from social media or television or text messages from friends and coworkers, we don't have a chance to be still and hear God's direction. We can't experience the refreshing He wants to do in our spirits.

"Very early in the morning, while it was still dark, Jesus got up, left the house and went off to a solitary place, where he prayed" (Mark 1:35). I have gone through seasons of waking up early and reading my Bible and praying before starting my day, and I have gone through seasons where I didn't spend the time I needed to spend with the Lord. During the times I wake up a little earlier and say, "Good morning, God. What do you want to talk to me about today?" I feel His presence. There is something about the early morning hours when the house is quiet and the sun is barely peeking out from behind the trees. In the silent beauty, I find my mind and heart more open to receive what God has to say to me.

Even when we are in tune with the Holy Spirit, we can't anticipate the needs of everyone. My husband and I try to be mindful of what is going on at work. If we are short-handed, we will oftentimes order lunch for everyone, so they don't have to leave the store to pick it up. It gives them extra time to actually relax and eat. One time I didn't order lunch, because I was going out of town and had a lot going on. I caught wind of an employee who made the comment, "Well, they should have paid for our lunch today." The words stung. I felt like I was doing all I could do. I felt so bad I didn't anticipate the need, until I realized I shouldn't have to anticipate every need of grown adults. They all knew the schedule ahead of time, and they could have chosen to bring their lunch or made plans. As leaders, we can do all we can to take care of people and still miss the mark. However, we can't put pressure on ourselves to try and meet everyone's needs, especially when we are working with adults. We can't always be

8 LEADING WITH JESUS

responsible for how people feel about us.

Once I hired a young girl. She seemed nice, but she wasn't the best employee. She was late a lot and made many mistakes. I spoke to her calmly about her mistakes, and tried to communicate my appreciation of her hard work, while pointing out the need for her to be on time. I asked her to pay closer attention to detail so she wouldn't make as many mistakes. From my viewpoint, the conversation with her went well. It seemed like things were going in a positive direction until she called in sick during one of our busiest weeks. I explained to her how much we needed her there, but she ended up calling in sick again the next day. She even told another employee she wanted to leave us in a bind. I felt as if I had been slapped in the face. I had to realize I can't fix people's attitudes. What people say about us says even more about them most of the time. In this case, I knew we had done what we could to help her be successful.

Sometimes as Christian leaders, we think we have to make everyone happy and always say, "yes." I have to admit I am naturally a people-pleaser. I always want to say yes whenever possible. There have been many times I worked in someone's place when I had other things to do, because I wanted the person to be able to attend a child's school event or take a last-minute trip with a friend. I think we should do those things for our team members when we can, but we also have to be okay with saying no and knowing it doesn't make us a bad person. It's like parenting, sometimes you have to say no for the good of the family. Sometimes you have to say no so your leadership style is consistent and trusted. Anytime I think about saying yes to something where I usually give a no answer, I have to filter it through many questions like: Is this fair? Will this set a precedent I don't want to set? What if this was a different employee, would my response be the same?

There will be many times our team members don't agree with our decisions, and that's okay. I am known for allowing them to have input into some decisions, but I also have to be careful as to not ask for input into issues in which they don't have the big picture. It's not fair to them or us to involve them in some of those decisions. It's important that we explain why we do what we do when we can, but we can't be responsible for their feelings towards us and our decisions. I like the adage, "What someone else thinks of me is not my business." It's the truth. It is impossible to make 100 percent of people happy. Sometimes our people will be happy with us, and sometimes they will be angry at us. It's okay! The sooner we accept this, the better we will sleep at night.

It's important to look at Jesus and His example found in Matthew. *"Now Jesus stood before the governor, and the governor asked him, "Are you the King of the Jews?" Jesus said, "You have said so." But when he was accused by the chief priests and elders, he gave no answer. Then Pilate said to him, "Do you not hear how many things they testify against you?" But he gave him no answer, not even a single charge, so that the governor was greatly amazed"* (Matthew 27:11-14). As people, we often feel the need to over explain ourselves to others in an attempt to minimize our fear, guilt or self-doubt. It's important that we allow God to mold us into the leader he wants us to be. We need to be able to walk in His courage, strength and boldness. That's impossible if we aren't connected to Jesus, the Vine, every single day.

Our job as leaders is to make the best decisions we can in making the companies we run successful. No one is going to know what it feels like to be in your shoes until they are. Sometimes I will ask team members, especially ones I am training for a management role, "How would you have handled situation xyz?" It really helps him/her to empathize with you for a moment and see the kind of difficulties experienced in a managerial role.

It's okay for your team members to see you as a person who experiences emotions, too. However, it's important that we learn to control our emotions to avoid acting out and regretting it later. Jesus was not defensive in his interactions. In Mark, chapter 10, James and John actually say to Jesus, "We want you to do for us whatever we ask." Can you imagine saying that to Jesus? I am pretty sure I have had team members who felt that way about us. Overstepping a boundary much? However, Jesus didn't seem bothered by this comment. His security came from God. He didn't need people's approval. He was about his Father's business. So why do we beat ourselves up so much when we don't please people with our leadership decisions?

People can be demanding, and ask us for more than we can give. We can bring more stress upon ourselves trying to please the masses. And, in case you haven't noticed, the masses can't be pleased. When we had our flood disaster, we had people who were upset with us because we couldn't fulfill their floral requests that week. Can you believe that? Well, if you are a leader, you probably can. Literally, our store and merchandise had been sitting under two feet of water for several days, and a customer was upset with us. We also had people openly comment about being happy the flood had happened, because they were getting good deals on some of our salvageable merchandise. It's in these moments we have to consider the source, and consider the sin in the world, which comes with selfishness and, well, let's face it, a little craziness thrown in!

WE INSTEAD OF YOU

A lot of what we say to people is judged by them based on how we said it, instead of what we said. It's important to pay attention to our tone, body language and mannerisms when we speak to customers or team members. Using "we" language instead of "you" and "me" language is also helpful. There have been a number of times when I have walked up on a situation or conversation without all of the facts. At first, based on what I saw on the surface, I would feel angry or like someone wasn't doing what was supposed to be done. I have learned to stop and ask questions first. Questions like: "Can you tell me what you're working on?", "Is there something you need to finish this particular project?", or "Is there something I can do to help you accomplish your tasks?" A lot of the time, the employee has good intentions and is working on a task. Maybe you just happened to walk up at an inopportune moment or maybe the team member is taking some time to think about how to proceed. Sometimes you find they need help, but didn't want to ask.

When our team members see us as approachable and caring, they are more likely to feel comfortable asking for help. One of the worst things we can do is ask questions like: "What are you doing?", "Why aren't you doing xyz?", or "You should be doing abc instead of xyz." We must first seek to understand before responding and possibly overreacting. If a team member is breaking the cell phone policy, for example, I ask them if something is going on at home and work with them on a temporary plan to help them work through it. We have to remember our team members are people who have families and issues. This doesn't mean they get to consistently or constantly break the rules, but we have to take into consideration their humanness and work with them when we can. Some team members can handle more freedom than others, but it's hard to allow some to not follow a rule while others have to follow the rule.

EXERCISE

1. Do you have boundaries with people you work with or manage? Why or why not? Take time to list some of the healthy boundaries you have in place to protect your sanity, heart, and energy.

2. Where are areas in which better boundaries are needed in your

8 LEADING WITH JESUS

life? Take time to write them down so you can recognize when they are being crossed. For example, is an employee or coworker constantly sucking the life out of you with dramatic conversations? This could be an area in which you need a better boundary.

3. When was the last time you said, 'yes' when you should have said no? How can you practice saying no in the future so you don't overtax yourself and your resources?

Chapter Nine

DECISIONS, DECISIONS, DECISIONS

One of the most challenging parts of leadership is the mountain of decisions that need to be made on a daily basis. Leaders are constantly bombarded with questions to the point of making our brains hurt. Since David and I lead together, I am fortunate that I can defer to him if I am feeling overwhelmed by decisions. It's good to have a partner, whether a spouse or business partner, to mull things over with and think about all of the pros and cons that come with any decision made. A good business partner is a goldmine. I can't tell you the number of times David and I have been able to help one another make good decisions based on different experiences and perspectives. I have strengths and weaknesses, and so does he. We know the areas where each of us is strong, and we allow that person to lead in their areas of strength. It's a give and take.

I have noticed I make two kinds of decisions, Jesus decisions and Jennifer decisions. When I make Jesus decisions by doing what God has told me to do, my life is more peaceful. I am equipped with His "yes," and I have the capacity and the grace to finish what He has called me to without losing my mind.

When I make Jennifer decisions, I end up feeling frazzled,

9 LEADING WITH JESUS

stressed and crazy. Just because I can does not mean I should. Maybe you can relate. I have learned the hard way decisions made out of pure emotions don't tend to fair very well. Jeremiah says, *"The heart is deceitful above all things and beyond cure. Who can understand it"* (Jeremiah 17:9)? Some of the worst decisions are made when people are stressed and frustrated, and emotions are running high.

For example, I have hired people out of a place of exhaustion and desperation. Once, when I couldn't imagine adding a single more to-do to my long list of "have-tos," I hired someone quickly. We were short-staffed and I was working a lot of extra hours filling in for people who had quit or didn't show up on time. I was also trying to take care of my job duties and crushing responsibilities. The exhaustion was crippling. I wanted a quick fix, pronto! I interviewed a few candidates for the position, and I settled on someone who wasn't qualified. At this point, I just wanted a warm body in the spot so I could regain some semblance of my sanity. I didn't pray very much about who to hire. Maybe I threw up a quick desperate plea, which I believe God can hear, but I didn't take time to listen to His response.

There are occasions when time is of the essence, and you don't have a lot of quiet moments. For us, this happened after the flood. A few months after the flood, we sat in the accountant's office taking a look at the grim financial state of the business following the loss. We had to make so many fast decisions, but God had grace for us and understood our circumstances. It felt as though He supernaturally increased our spiritual hearing so we wouldn't miss Him in the chaos. He was opening doors and making a way swiftly, and He was providing us peace in the process. You have to trust Him to give you the answers you need when you need them.

Sometimes we do all the talking without stopping to allow Him to speak into our situations. This one-sided approach doesn't work out well. I have learned it is worth waiting on the right person and trusting

God to give me the capacity to do what needs to be done while I wait on His timing. I have to remember He works all things out for my good…but He also works all things out for "her" good and "His" good, so my temporary suffering may mean, ultimately, getting the right person for the job. Never hire out of a place of desperation. Never sign up for a new software system without careful research, asking all the questions, reading all the fine print. Never make financial decisions without prayer. Never. Can you tell I am a bit traumatized?

Thankfully, I have learned I don't always make the best decisions on my own. In fact, my husband agrees and he feels the same way about himself. It may seem crazy that two people who aren't confident in their decision making abilities are in charge of a couple of businesses. It seems crazy to me! However, because we see this as a weakness, God is able to show up and show out when we lean on Him for instruction and direction. In 2 Corinthians 12:9-11, it says, *"But he said to me, 'My grace is sufficient for you, for my power is made perfect in weakness.' Therefore I will boast all the more gladly about my weaknesses, so that Christ's power may rest on me."*

We are actually supposed to boast about our weaknesses. I definitely boasted after the flood admitting to God I didn't know what to do except keep moving forward until He stopped me. I took the Strengths Finder Test, (because I am obsessed with personality assessments) and I discovered my top five strengths, with responsibility being my number one strength. When I operate in the realms of my strengths, it's a natural process. It is easy for me to take all the credit for my strengths, thinking it's all me. Yet, when I inspect the bottom five strengths, I find I am not self-assured and in these areas I struggle with making confident decisions. That's where God and His Holy Spirit come into play. The Holy Spirit is sent as our Helper. He will lead us and guide us on the right path when we link arms with Him and ask Him for directions. *"But the Helper, the Holy Spirit, whom the Father will send in my name, he will teach you all*

9 LEADING WITH JESUS

things and bring to your remembrance all that I have said to you."
(John 14:26)

GATE CHANGES

I traveled out of town to North Carolina to attend a conference. After the conference was over and my bags were packed, I caught a cab to the airport. Since I am a paranoid planner, I arrived the suggested two hours ahead of time to make sure I smoothly maneuvered my way through security and found my gate. I was dropped off at terminal A but had to walk to terminal E which seemed forever away.

I decided to be stubborn and not check any bags; therefore, I broke a sweat dragging two rather large bags through the airport. Not pretty.

I walked. And walked. And walked.
When I finally saw the glorious E gate, I sighed with relief. I overheard a lady with a small child say to another lady, "We need to walk to A. It's probably not that far."

I laughed and said to them, "It's a good fifteen minute walk from here."

"Really?" they asked.

"Yep." I replied, a little winded.

I knew it was none of my business, but I felt like preparing them for their lengthy and sweaty journey was the right thing to do. After all, they had a toddler in a stroller. Bless them. I silently thanked God that I didn't have a toddler in a stroller in the airport.

I walked onward to find a seat near my gate and rest my arm that felt like it would fall off from dragging all my luggage.

I settled in to an end spot, texted my husband that I had made it to my gate, and pulled out a new book I had purchased and began reading.

A lady with a thick Australian accent kept interrupting my reading with announcements about flight delays and gate changes.

People sighed and shifted in their seats. Some were standing ready to board their flight and began looking around the airport for a place to sit down.

Their plane was delayed. I was relieved, "Thank you, God, that it wasn't mine."

I kept checking the bright blue monitor for any changes that might negatively affect me.

I was more than ready to get home to see my husband and boys. Again, more announcements about delays. This time, the lady informed us that two planes were set to arrive at the same gate at the same time since one was late and one was on time. She instructed us all to be listening for a possible gate change.

I texted my husband, "Looks like I may be delayed. Maybe a gate change (Insert frowny face emoji)."

He replied, "It has happened to me so many times. Be ready to run in case it's in a different place."
Great, I thought to myself. I just got here and I may be running back to where I was.

I sat there listening and praying that I would board my flight on time without any gate changes.

It was in that moment that the Holy Spirit spoke to me about how changing directions and gate changes could be compared to what we sometimes walk out in our obedience to Him. I felt His gentleness as He used what I was experiencing to illustrate the way He works in our lives.

It's amazingly simple. He gives us a destination and we set out on our way. We walk and walk and walk dragging our luggage with tired arms. We encounter people who need us to encourage them and prepare them for their journey. We have walked from point A to point E, in my case, so we have some insight to offer — if we are willing to

9 LEADING WITH JESUS

share the way.

When we get to where we are going, we have to be prepared for what God has for us. There might be a delay. We may make it to our gate long before the plane is ready to depart. That doesn't mean the plane won't depart. It simply means that waiting is part of our journey. It might require us settling into our seat with the good Book, and patient anticipation.

Above all, it always requires us to listen. We must listen to His instructions, just like the passengers in the airport that day who listened to the lady with an Australian accent. We must listen for gate changes, and we must be prepared to pick up our bags and move again and again, if necessary, no matter how tired our arms feel from the perils of our journey.

Thankfully, my flight was unaffected on that particular day. I was at the right gate, waiting on the right plane, that would ultimately deliver me safely to my family at the right time.

Sometimes, you may find yourself in the middle of a transition or a change. You see people all around you seemingly getting to where they are going much faster. Perhaps you can't see how you will ever make it. It can be so hard to know what to do and when to do it. You are continuously trying to make big decisions about your health, job, family, church, and life.

It's in these moments of waiting that listening is so important. If you are tuned-in daily to the Heavenly Father, he won't let you miss your gate change, and He definitely won't let you miss the flight that will deliver you to where He wants you to be when He wants you to be there. You cannot underestimate the power of prayer. I have mentioned it in almost every chapter of this book, because it is incredibly important. It should be an item on your to-do list every day. Maybe you feel like you are not being productive if you aren't planning meetings, setting up promotions or events, replying to emails, returning the important phone calls, or seeing clients, but please listen

DECISIONS, DECISIONS, DECISIONS

to me when I say, you aren't being productive if you aren't praying. Setting aside time to pray for your team members, other leaders, and those pedaling in the same direction as you is imperative. How much time each week do you spend doing things verses praying about things? Most of us, myself included, need to make more time for conversations with the Father. I would go so far as to recommend, during the really difficult moments, finding a quiet retreat for a day or two in order to welcome God's voice into your hectic life. We sometimes have to change our scenery and daily habits to hear more clearly what God is saying to us. He is fully capable of speaking to us amongst the chaos and grind, but at times, He wants to be alone with you.

You can start by writing down the names of all of those serving with you or who are also a part of the project. Pray over each person, asking God to reveal to you anything He wants you to know about the people involved and the situation you're facing. Thank God for what He has already done for you in the past. Now take time to pray specifically about the hard decisions you are trying to make. Give the Lord a chance to shed light on darkness and bring order to the chaotic thoughts racing around in your brain. Ask God to reign in your emotions and plans and bring His peace and His plan. Ask Him to give you patience through the process. Explain to Him, and mean it, you don't want to miss Him and His will.

WORD AND SPIRIT

When it comes to decision-making, you have to be aware of the emotions you are bringing to the table. As previously stated Jeremiah 17:9 tells us, *"The heart is deceitful above all things; and desperately sick; who can understand it?"* I don't think a lot of people stop to acknowledge this verse in our "follow your heart," world. Stop following your heart. Instead, follow Jesus and His infallible Word.

9 LEADING WITH JESUS

You can't allow your emotions and heart to take control while pushing Jesus to the back row of your life and work. If you want the fruits of Jesus, you have to be willing to surrender your thoughts, your emotions, and your entire life to Him. Like an airplane, your heart can take you for a ride; taking off with hope and quickly descending when clouds of doubt appear. You have to remember your heart can lie to you. In fact, your heart will lie to you. Your emotions can't be trusted. You have to be careful about making emotional decisions that can cause long-term damage. Unless absolutely necessary, avoid making major decisions quickly taking time to discover the big picture and long lasting effects once the ink has dried or the words have been said. Slow and steady are the character traits that win the race. In the book of Jeremiah, you'll find, *"I the Lord search the heart and test the mind, give every man according to his ways, according to the fruits of his deeds"* (Jeremiah 17:10). The Lord knows your heart better than you know your heart. He knows your innermost thoughts, and He knows the motivations behind every decision you make. When you make decisions based on His Word, He can bless you beyond measure.

You have to have a balance of Word and Spirit in your decision making abilities. The Word is given to you as a tool and resource, but it requires the Holy Spirit to come alongside you, through faith, to give you revelation. Every answer to every question is found in God's Word and through His awesome Spirit. However, you have to ask God what He wants for you, and you have to do the work of reading scriptures in an effort to discover His answers. There are no shortcuts. Unfortunately, we often ask Him as a last resort. Sometimes instead of going to Him first, I find myself trying to problem-solve, research, ask opinions, and talk an issue to death with other people; however God wants us to talk to Him first. Our faith is relationship-based. Intimate time with the Creator of the Universe brings clarity and understanding to any situation.

You may be saying, "Well, I have asked Him for an answer, and He still hasn't given it to me." I wish I had a clear-cut answer for you, friend. All I can tell you is that you have to keep asking, taking it step-by-step, day-by-day, and year-by-year. You have to trust Him to open the right doors and close the wrong ones. His revelations can come in one fell swoop or gradually unfold inch by painful inch.

Since the flood, we have had to make a lot of quick decisions. Typically, I am a slow and steady decision maker. I have taken years to make a decision before, because I felt like I shouldn't move until I was absolutely sure I was making the right call. But when your livelihood is threatened by flood waters, you either sink or swim. We decided to swim, especially since God seemed to be opening doors and providing a way out for us. After a couple of days of cleaning up and wrapping our minds around what we were facing, David and I knew we were going to have to make difficult decisions. Our decisions would either help us survive or our brick and mortar would be left an unrecovered mess. Within a few days, we secured a new location for our store and began moving everything not damaged by the flood to the new location. We also had a flood sale in our parking lot to unload damaged merchandise. Some of the merchandise just needed some tender love and care to be back to a normal state. Customers were lined up waiting for us to cut the yellow caution tape so they could purchase what was left behind. We made each decision minute-by-minute, hour-by-hour, and day-by-day. The planner in me was stretched immensely. I always like to know months in advance what life is going to look like, but during this time, it was just me trusting God day-in and day-out in all areas of my life. Not only were we in recovery mode for our business, but we still had obligations outside of work to our family, church and community. It is only through God's grace I am here to write these words to you and not in bed with my head under the covers refusing to press forward. A lot of people say, "Everything happens for a reason." I actually think I may have had

9 LEADING WITH JESUS

that quote under my picture in my high school yearbook at some point. However, the longer I live, the more I understand that not all things happen for a reason. Some things happen because we live in a fallen world. We have free will to make decisions, which reap consequences. Sometimes we fall victim to natural disasters. I don't believe God sent the flood waters upon us, but I do believe He knew we would use our situation for His good and to bring glory to His name. I knew I was right where I was supposed to be as I took out loads and loads of ruined products to our city garbage bin. No matter what your leadership role looks like, you have probably asked God some tough questions about where He has placed you, and maybe you have even questioned if He truly placed you there.

THE STORY OF ESTHER

Are you where you believe God has placed you? Has He been speaking to you about your purpose and your place? Do you remember the story of Esther? It's a hard one to forget. But to jog your memory, the King chooses Esther out of all the women to be Queen not knowing that she was a Jew. *"The king loved Esther more than all the women, and she found favor and kindness with him"* (Esther 2:17).

The story of Esther is one of my favorites. She uses her influence, courage and intelligence to save her people. When my husband and I were serving as interim youth pastors at our church, I completed a Bible study on Esther with the girls. We dug deep into the story and what it meant to be Esther *"for such a time as this"* (Esther 4:14). The story demonstrates God's love and sovereignty. At a time when Jews were being exiled, persecuted and killed, God planted Esther inside the castle as His secret weapon. She won over the King and ultimately preserved her bloodline.

How in the world did she do this? At first, Esther didn't want to go along when all the girls in the kingdom were summoned by the

King. She begged her cousin, "Please don't make me." But in the end, Esther was obedient. She wanted to please her cousin, who had authority over her, and follow his instructions. She trusted his decision to send her.

In life and business, it can be very important to have trustworthy advisors who have our best in mind helping us along our journey. Esther's cousin, Mordecai, knew what was best for her, and she placed her trust in him. Can you imagine being Esther? She was young and being summoned to go meet a strange man. I think most of us would be terrified and intimidated. It's so much responsibility. I imagine her not feeling ready. I can imagine her cousin, Mordecai, giving her words of wisdom, "Esther, you mustn't pray for just what you want, but for what God wants." I don't know that those were his exact words, but I can hear him encouraging her and reminding her what she was doing was for a greater cause. I can't fathom the amount of pressure and stress she must have felt as she carried out this larger than life purpose.

I began thinking about all the people who were born at "the right time." What if Michaelangelo had been born one hundred years earlier? Art was not important or appreciated then, but he lived through the Renaissance, and is still revered as one of the greatest artists of all time.

What if J.J. Thompson hadn't discovered the electron some twenty years before Einstein was born? Would Einstein have had the building blocks necessary to form the Theory of Relativity? I don't know. Maybe, maybe not.

I think about all the local musicians I know who have the ability to self-publish music. Not just good music, but great music. If they were born fifty years ago, would anyone have ever heard their music? If not for blogs and social media outlets, how many writers would never have eyes to see their work? I think of myself and this wonderful thing called the internet, where I can pick apart my life and pour out

9 LEADING WITH JESUS

my fears leaving a little of my story with each reader in the hopes of encouraging someone or making people feel less alone.

PURPOSE AND DREAMS

You see, God doesn't make mistakes. In Jeremiah 1:5, God says, *"Before I formed you in the womb I knew you, before you were born I set you apart; I appointed you as a prophet to the nations."* Granted, God was talking to Jeremiah in this verse; however, he knows us all before we were knitted together in the womb. He has a purpose for our lives, a destiny. And if we are listening to Him, He won't let our indecisiveness or poor mistakes made in good faith keep us from getting to where He is sending us. Obedience doesn't mean we won't endure hardships or suffering along the journey. Remember Joseph being sent to prison for something he didn't do? He was such an asset to Pharaoh and Pharaoh's kingdom. He interpreted dreams and walked in God's wisdom. But Pharaoh's wife accused him of trying to sexually attack her, and he was thrown in jail and forgotten by man. I'm sure Joseph was very frustrated and possibly feeling like he was wasting his talents and giftings in prison. But he seized the opportunity and fed fellow prisoners. Little did he know, God was preparing him to feed the nations. Eventually, Pharaoh needed someone to interpret his dreams, and he called for Joseph. Joseph was able to tell Pharaoh the meaning of the dreams which helped Pharaoh prepare for the famine keeping the people from starving. (Genesis 40:1-41) There will be times in our lives we feel captives of a proverbial prison, but it doesn't mean it's over or that God is finished with us. In fact, He has a reputation of setting the captives free – that includes you and me!

Purpose is fulfilled through one small act of obedience at a time. Our purpose has to be bigger than our wants. Esther knew that becoming queen was about something more than a position in the kingdom. Do you realize what God has called you to do is something more than a position and a title? Do you really want the work and sacrifice that comes with ministry outside the walls of the church? Do you want your business to be your ministry? Those are important questions to ask yourself daily. But I hope you will find the answer is "YES," because we have been called Christ bearers and have a duty to share the gospel wherever we find ourselves. You must trust God to equip you and place you where He wants you when He wants you there.

Most people have dreams. Dreams keep us motivated, and they keep us pressing forward. They keep hope alive inside of us, yet how many of those dreams point back to Jesus? In a world beckoning us to be a better parent, a better spouse, a better leader, and a better version of ourselves, we forget our goal should be getting ourselves out of the way and looking more like Jesus.

At the end of the day, it's not about our profit and loss statement, how much money we made, what sales looked like for the year, what car we drove, what vacation we took, how many followers we have on social media, or where our kids went to school. I don't believe God will ask about those things when we meet Him in heaven.

I can; however, hear Him asking me, "Child, how many people did you share my love with? How many people did you introduce my Son to? You were born for the time in which you lived. I gave you all the resources you needed to win people to me. Did you use your time and energy to advance my Kingdom? Did you allow me to help you make decisions?"

FRESH START

When we experienced #floodpocalypse in our businesses, we had been praying for God to show up in a mighty way and guide us. I'm not saying God flooded our business, but because of the flood, some of our problems were solved, and we had to start over in a lot

9 LEADING WITH JESUS

of areas. Sometimes, we need a fresh start. We need time to purge and get rid of the messes that some of our less than great decisions have gotten us into. We have to extend grace to ourselves. We aren't perfect people, and we can't make perfect decisions. I'm always the girl with plan A, B, and C, but when we experienced the flooding, I didn't have a plan. We were told by the insurance agency as well as others who had experienced flooding in their lifetimes, "You really can't plan for this kind of thing. You have to take it day-by-day."

I'm reminded of Exodus 40:36, *"So the cloud of the Lord was over the tabernacle by day, and fire was in the cloud by night, in the sight of all the house of Israel during all their travels."*

I find myself wanting answers, and I want them now. Have you ever felt that way? I want to know what God's plan is for me five years from now. I think, "God, if you would just tell me, I will do whatever is needed to get there. I want to make you proud." I forget that God is already proud of me just as I am. He loves me for who I am in Him and not for what I can do for Him. God calls us, His people, His "bride," not His maid. There is nothing you or I can do to make Him love us any more or any less.

Even though I am aware of His love, I feel like we live in a world of impatience and instant gratification. Why do I have to wait? I don't like to wait. I want to have a plan. Just give me the plan, and I will make it happen. Yes, I know, God has ordered my steps and is in control of my path, but sometimes I want Him to speed things along. I can be pretty foolish. If He told me the whole plan ahead of time, I probably wouldn't get any rest trying to make it come together overnight. I can be obsessive, compulsive, and impatient.

There have been many times in my life I have prayed for direction. I have asked God, probably to the point of annoying Him, what He wants me to do. I have wagered with Him and promised Him I would do whatever He asks me to do if He would reveal His plan to me. I usually don't get a flashing sign. Nor do I hear His gentle voice nudging me in one direction or another. The silence can be deafening and frustrating.

I like to think God and I are buds. We talk on a regular basis. He speaks life into my soul. He encourages me, but sometimes when I ask Him about particular life decisions, including business decisions, He's dead quiet. Every day, I ask. I persist. Sometimes I beg and grovel. I threaten to never ask again, cross my arms, stomp my foot, stick out my bottom lip, and get a little bull-headed. See, I told you I can be foolish. But just like it doesn't work with me when my children do those things, this behavior doesn't work with God when I do those things.

I can almost hear His voice, "Go ahead, big girl. Stomp all you want. It's not time for you to know my plan, yet."

When I hear nothing, I change my attitude, approach His throne as humble as I know how, and ask again, "Is it time yet, Lord? I'm sorry for being a brat yesterday."

THE ISRAELITES AND US

While reading my Bible looking for revelation, I stumbled upon Exodus and began to see so many similarities that can be applied to my situation. I think you might find them applicable to your situation, as well.

As you may recall, the Israelites were laboring as slaves day-in and day-out under the piercing heat of the Egyptian sun. I can picture them with aching backs, sweaty brows and dusty bruised up knuckles. The people were carrying a heavy burden, beaten up, and in need of a Redeemer to set them free from bondage. I can imagine one Israelite looking towards his neighbor with saddened eyes pleading, "There has to be more to life than this." I can hear the equally frustrated neighbor saying, "Where is this Yahweh? Why isn't He saving us?"

9 LEADING WITH JESUS

Can you relate to any of this so far? Maybe you are tired of making decisions on your own. Maybe you are tired of thinking God isn't showing up and guiding you like you would like. Be honest. Maybe some of us aren't physically beaten down, but we are emotionally and spiritually exhausted. We are trying to do this "Jesus in the marketplace" thing well, and we feel like we are failing. We might be asking, "Lord, where are you? I long to hear from you, but I am still a slave to this leadership problem, this relationship problem, this business problem, this financial problem…" and the list continues. God could have easily lowered His mighty hand and knocked the Pharaoh to the ground, freeing the Israelites. He could have literally lowered the boom and fixed all of their problems. Isn't that exactly what we want Him to do for us?

But Exodus 7:5 says, *"And the Egyptians will know that I am the Lord when I stretch out my hand against Egypt and bring the Israelites out."* God cared just as much for the Egyptians as He did for the Israelites. You see, it's not always about us. God wanted to show them His power through their circumstances. Soak that up a minute. God cared just as much for the pagan, false-god-worshipping, rotten Egyptians as He did for His chosen people, the Israelites. He wanted them all to know Him.

God kept His word and finally freed the Israelites, delivering them into the land of milk and honey. We often feel like we aren't living in the promised land. We can get so caught up in our circumstances instead of claiming the ground we have already gained. We allow thoughts of the enemy and people to steal our peace and joy. Satan wants us to live in defeat. It's his grand scheme. He wants to keep us discouraged and lowly. He wants us to feel like we are never going to make it to our promised land. He wants us to believe God isn't going to answer us so we might as well take matters into our own hands. We can make the best decisions possible and still not have it made in the shade. Being successful doesn't always equate to all of our problems being solved and life being blue skies and sandy beaches. There will be trials and tribulations until our dying breath, but there will also be a sovereign God holding our hand as we journey onward.

During the Israelites' travels, God sent a cloud to cover them. It was a communication device from the Father, reminding them to sit still. When He lifted the cloud, it was their cue to move.

Like the Israelites, I think God sometimes parks the same kind of cloud over us and our situation. Sometimes the cloud is for our own protection, sometimes it is to teach us something like faith, patience and trust. It can also be for us to spend more time communicating with Him. And sometimes, it has nothing to do with us. Shocking, huh? Sometimes He is using us and our circumstances to teach someone else about His awesome love, power and mercy. If we really want to make a difference in our world, we need to be okay with that.

Mark Batterson's book, *Circle Maker*, is a great book about prayer. He urges us to write our prayers down and then circle the prayer each time we pray about it. It calls attention to how much time we are spending communicating with the Father about our requests. I may think I am praying enough about a situation or for a particular person, but when I make a physical note of the prayer request and circle it each time I pray, I can be embarrassed about how little I have truly prayed.

Whatever situation you find yourself in as you read these words, know that God still cares. Whatever concerns you concern Him. He still loves you. Listen to Him. Don't stop asking for guidance. Don't stop being obedient. Be ready to move when He tells you to move and sit still when you don't hear Him. He is still orchestrating, like only He can, your exodus, or exit, out of the current bondage in which you find yourself. He is never late. He is always on time. You matter to Him. The desires of your heart, the ones He gave you, matter to Him. He knows you don't desire to struggle with what to do and when to do it.

God remembered the Israelites, and He remembers you. God is

9 LEADING WITH JESUS

wise. He is good at His job. Stop making willy-nilly decisions on your own because you haven't heard from Him. An omnipotent, Almighty wants to give you the answers you need to make solid, life-changing, center-of-His-will decisions. Jesus depended on God for answers, and if we want to be like Jesus to those around us, we have to depend on Him, too. Keep camping under His cloud of protection until He moves you.

EXERCISE

1. Have your decisions been covered in prayer?

2. Have you allowed the Holy Spirit to come alongside you and help you with the decisions you are making or are you doing it all on your own?

3. When we are in the middle of God's will, we will experience His favor. It doesn't mean everything is easy, but we will see God open doors and move mountains. When we are not in His favor, we can experience roadblock after roadblock. Recount some times God has worked in your favor. Write down these experiences so you can remember them later when times get hard. Where have you experienced roadblock after roadblock?

4. Have you made time to listen to God after you have prayed? When can you commit to doing so?

Chapter Ten

CRAVING GREATNESS

As I was washing the baseboards in my bathroom, I was dreaming about things I want to do in the future. With each stroke of my scrubbing brush against the grain of the wood, I thought of the ministry work I want to do, how I would do it, and why I want to do it. I was deep in thought when my son, who was four at the time, asked, "Can I help?" My train of thought was broken as I handed him a cloth and said, "Sure, you can help." He only lasted about a minute before saying, "I'm tired and want to go play."

I started thinking about how hard we work and how we sometimes forget the most important things. We forget to keep dreaming, and to keep playing. We forget to take it easy and enjoy those around us. As leaders, we crave greatness. We want to make a difference in our home, in our family, in our job, and in our leadership roles, whether they be at work or church. Leaders usually have the capacity to handle a lot of things at one time, but it comes with a price.

At some point, you are going to crash if you aren't careful. There will be areas in your life in which you feel you could have done more. Maybe you are killing it at work, but you aren't the best spouse you could be. Maybe you have met all of your goals for the month, but you

10 LEADING WITH JESUS

aren't spending as much time with your kids as they need. You stay up late trying to accomplish as much as possible. Personally, working full-time, while being a Mom with a husband who travels and works late hours, can leave me dancing solo at times. This solo act keeps me from connecting with friends, because I am in survival mode. So many times I have planned to have families over to grill burgers and swim, but I don't get around to extending the invite before summer says, "See yah." Then, I feel guilty for not hosting my friends and showing them a good time. I put an extreme amount of pressure on myself to do it all and be it all. A lot of the time what holds me back is not feeling like my house looks spotless or my pool area is as pristine as it can be; rather it's an attitude of perfectionism. I find I always want to be great at everything I do. Can you relate to the achiever mentality?

If you are like me, most of the pressure you carry is pressure you have heaped upon yourself. You set the bar higher and higher as you are motivated by achievements. You want to do something so ambitious and so meaningful that you inadvertently miss the little moments to be great. These little moments are the ones that matter the most. If you have children, teaching your children about Christ is one of the highest callings in your life. If you are doing that, then guess what? You are being great. If you love and respect your spouse, you are doing something great. When you take food to a friend, who just had surgery, you are doing something great. If you honor your father and mother, you are doing something great. If you make it a point to seek out the loneliest person in the room and strike up a conversation, you are fulfilling the call to be great. You are being the hands and feet of Jesus in these moments. It's your purpose and what you were created to do. What could be greater?

I have come to the realization that I don't want my life to be so full and busy with activities that I don't have time for what really matters: studying the Word, developing my personal relationship with Jesus,

CRAVING GREATNESS 10

being there for my family and friends, and taking time to slow down and show the love of my Savior to the world. I don't need to be busy to feel important. One way to combat the temptation to be perpetually achieving is to turn your "I want to do" statements into "I want to be" statements. Watch how your perspective changes. For example, instead of "I want to sell a million dollars worth of products this year," say, "I want to be a person of integrity who shows Jesus and His love wherever I go." Sure, measurable goals are required in life. In fact, they are excellent, but when your identity begins to be tethered to the outcomes rather than the person you are becoming in the process, you can miss what the Lord has for you.

Rest in the fact that you are a son or daughter of the Most High, and He has commanded you, above all, to love others just as Christ has loved us (John 13:34-35). Don't be so busy striving to achieve greatness that you forget to smile and say, 'hi' to a stranger. Don't forget to slow down long enough to spend time with your family and friends.

DIVINE APPOINTMENTS

A while ago, David slowed down long enough to love a homeless man in Atlanta, Georgia. He was visiting Atlanta to set up our permanent showroom at America's Mart. It's a daunting task which requires hours of work and long days and nights. He is always racing against the clock to finish the work. I remember the phone call well, "I had lunch with a homeless man today," he told me. "I'm walking back to the market right now, but I thought I would call and let you know."

"What?" I asked in surprise. I knew he was racing against the clock to get work done, so I was kind of surprised he had taken time to even eat lunch. He's notorious for skipping meals. He is also notorious for being an introvert. He has learned to act like an extrovert in business settings, but in his heart of hearts, he can be a total loner.

10 LEADING WITH JESUS

I have always joked with him that he missed his calling of working for the CIA. Talking to strangers is not in his nature or comfort zone. His need for people is a little lower than mine; although, he has been realizing more and more the value of connectedness.

He continued, "Yeah, I saw this guy on the side of the street. He told me he didn't want any money, but he asked if I could get him some food. He told me he was hungry."

"Wow!" I was listening.

I assumed my husband, who was generous, bought him a meal and sent him on his way. Generosity is one of his strong suits even if conversations aren't.

"We stood in line together at Chick-Fil-A and talked. After we got our food, I asked him if he would sit down and eat with me. He agreed."

"Wait, you sat down with a total stranger and ate lunch with him? I mean, that's awesome, but wow!" I was in awe. He continued to fill me in on his unexpected lunch, "I asked him what his story was, and he told me. He said he had not always lived like this. He explained to me that he had recently been released from jail because of a DUI, and he didn't have anywhere to go since his family had run out of grace for him."

"How sad," I choked out the words as tears filled my eyes.

"We talked for about an hour," he said. "I told him God had more for him than the life he was living, and that the people we surround ourselves with can help make or break us. I explained every decision has consequences and sometimes turning your life around has to do with making one good decision, then the next, and the next."

"That's amazing. What did he say?" I inquired.

David explained that this man's name was Remy and others had stopped to talk to him, but they had been less encouraging. Remy told David a Christian man stopped to talk to him earlier and told him he wasn't sure he would ever be able to change because his name,

Remy, was a brand of alcohol. It was as if this man was insinuating Remy was destined to be a drunkard based on his name.

I gasped. "How encouraging," retorting with sarcasm. David continued, "I told him God wanted to give him a new name, make him a new creation, and set his foot upon the Rock. I told him, God will totally transform his life, if he will seek God first in all things."

Now I couldn't even get a squeak out. I was so touched by the fact that my introverted husband had sat down and broken bread with a stranger and shared the gospel. He stopped chasing his goals, his dreams and his own greatness to spend a minute with someone who mattered to the Lord. He gave the good news to a guy with no hope, no truth and no Jesus.

"This was a divine appointment," I said.

"Yes, I believe it was. I told him my story and how God changed my life. I prayed for the man before I left him, and I gave him my cell phone number. He told me he didn't have a phone, but I told him to call me if he got one," David concluded.

The whole time he talked, I played it all out in my head hearing my husband's gentle voice talking to this desperate man. My husband was there on company business, but he took a minute to walk out what we preach all the time and be Jesus in the marketplace.

He was super busy on the day of the encounter, racing against the clock, but he realized building the kingdom of God was more important than building his own kingdom. Isn't that what Jesus is all about? Jesus was not known for hurrying through life chasing His own ambitions. He was about his Father's business. There doesn't seem to be a lot of instances in the Bible of Jesus rushing around. One time, He did command Zacchaeus, the tax collector, to quickly come down from the tree. *"Zacchaeus, make haste and come down, for I must stay at your house today"* (Luke 19:5). The people complained, *"He has gone to be a guest with a man who is a sinner"* (Luke 19:6). The only thing Jesus was in a hurry about in the story of Zacchaeus was bringing salvation to his house. He wasn't in a hurry to reach a financial, sales, or team goal. His goal was not to be nominated, "World's Greatest Boss," or to close a lucrative deal. He didn't care about the number of social media followers or likes on a post. He was, however, in a hurry to offer salvation to a despised sinner. If we are truly in the Jesus business, no matter what our day job looks like, we will take time for any Zacchaeuses God sends our way.

My husband has never been homeless, but he's been broken. He knows the difference God can make in a life. Our business is our mission field. We are nothing and would have nothing without God's grace, mercy and support. Our goal is to represent Christ everywhere our feet touch and gain ground for Jesus putting greatness and pride aside. We feel like God has tested us multiple times to make sure our motives are pure and our hearts are right.

God is able to embolden us to talk to strangers, and to share His unconditional love and unfailing mercy. He is able to change our circumstances and give us wisdom to make decisions that glorify Him. Our struggles in life are temporary, just like our leadership roles, but God's goodness is permanent. Even if we find ourselves without an earthly home and an upside down business, we can rest in knowing we have an eternal home with the Creator of it all. This is good news definitely worth sharing with others.

THE STORY OF SAMSON

One morning, my youngest son was listening to the story of Samson on his Kids Bible app while getting ready for school and I listened, too. In the story, Delilah nagged Samson until he told her the secret of his strength, *"No razor has ever been used on my head because I have been a Nazirite dedicated to God from my mother's womb. If my head were shaved, my strength would leave me, and I would become as weak as any other man"* (Judges 16:17). When I think of Samson, I get a mental image of a Fabio-looking character, all long-haired and muscular.

Delilah basically stroked Samson's hair until he fell asleep in her lap. She then called for men to take a razor to his head and shave him bald. He awoke, weak, and unable to free himself from their chains. It's just like the enemy to lull you to sleep and then take what is most important from you while binding you up in chains.

He didn't carry any actual strength in his lovely locks. He carried a promise given to him by God in his symbolic name, Samson. In Hebrew, Samson means "bright sun." Samson's story all boiled down to a test of obedience and faith. He failed. But guess what? The story didn't end there. It was merely getting started.

If you remember, God kept his promises to Samson, even though Samson didn't keep his promises to God. Samson cried out to God to strengthen him once more so he could shake, and ultimately destroy the Philistine walls, and God listened. Isn't it amazing how God's promises are not dependent upon us? We can make mistakes, but He can still make good things happen on our behalf. Walking in obedience and doing as He asks of us ensures His promises are fulfilled leading to a demonstration of His greatness and not ours.

If we never see our promises come to pass, I can guarantee that God is not the problem. We are the experts at messing things up, but when we repent, Jesus cleans up our messes. He will do what He says He is going to do. He will bring to pass what He has promised. He keeps His word when those around us don't. However, it's extremely important we make sure we are carrying a promise from God and not just our own preferences and ideas of how we would like things to be. We can feel like we are supposed to do something because it's all we have ever known or because we are skilled in a certain area. Maybe we prefer being our own boss, so we think it must be what God wants for us. Preferences are thoughts on how we think things should be, but promises from God are the way things should be.

We have a choice to either trust God to make good on the promises sewn into our hearts or not. It's simple, I believe. Can you relate to Samson? Has there been a promise Jesus has entrusted you with regarding your business or leadership role? Maybe you feel like you have made bad decisions or not kept your end of the deal. Is there something you cut off, but God asked you to keep it? Maybe there's something He has asked you to cut off, but you have kept it instead? Maybe you have tried to reach the destination on your own without consulting Him for wisdom and guidance. If so, it's okay. Just as Samson did, ask Him to help you start again and breathe life back into the promises He has given you. He is the ultimate promise keeper.

Samson got comfortable with Delilah. Maybe he thought his strength wouldn't be taken away given his track record. He could have begun to think of himself as a status symbol. If we are not careful, we can begin to make our position, our title, or our career paths a graven image. We can settle in and get comfortable. It can become the most important thing in our lives. It's important to identify what idols we may have in our lives. Let's first begin with defining what a modern day idol is. According to Google dictionary, an idol is "an image or representation of god used as an object of worship."

Maybe you're thinking, I don't have anything I worship more than God! I would challenge you to think about where your thoughts were this past week. Think about how many times you thought about God and His word verses how many times you thought about things contrary to God's word. Have you obeyed the Lord and His commandments or have you served yourself?

IDOLATRY

The Israelites in Exodus give us the best example of all that can go wrong when we have idols and false gods. It seems like a natural instinct for people to worship something or someone. The Israelites spent forty days in the wilderness. Every time they did what God told them to do, they seemed to do well. Once they began to worship false gods, everything went downhill.

Sometimes our biggest idols are ourselves. We are a culture obsessed with success, being known and recognized. We want people to remember us. We want to leave a legacy. Maybe dying seems easier if we think we won't be forgotten when we're gone. A lot of our thoughts throughout the day are about ourselves. Our culture promotes me, me, me! Isaiah 14:12-15 tells us the story of Satan when he challenged God. *"For you have said in your heart: I will ascend into heaven, I will exalt my throne above the stars of God; I will also sit on the mount of the congregation on the farthest sides of the north; I will ascend above the heights of the clouds, I will be like the Most High."* Notice how many times Satan used the word "I." How many times a day do we start our sentences with I? We can be self-centered by nature, without even realizing it.

This focus of self is a form of idolatry. Spending more time building your empire instead of God's kingdom is a form of idolatry. Worshiping celebrities, sports figures, famous preachers and other superstars is a form of idolatry. When things and people are able to shake our worlds to the core, we've found our idols.

We can combat idolatry with humility. It's okay to focus on our desires and God's promises to us, but we can't lose our identity in the process. We can't want the promise more than the Promise Keeper. We can't desire to exalt ourselves more than we exalt God. At the end of the day, our purpose and fulfillment should come from God. Our identity rests in Him alone. He calls us His sons and daughters. He calls us His masterpieces. He calls us out of the depths of self-absorption and despair and into His Kingdom. He calls us great.

10 LEADING WITH JESUS

EXERCISE

1. Do you have any idols in your life? If you aren't sure, think about what shakes your core when it doesn't go the way you think it should.

2. When was the last time you felt good about what you were doing? What were you doing during that moment? Are you fueled by man's applause or God's?

3. Is your work self-serving or are you taking the time to pour into others? When is the last time you recall making a difference in the lives of a coworker, employee, friend or stranger?

4. Look for an opportunity this week to serve someone in need. It could be giving a few dollars to the homeless man on the sidewalk, or encouraging an employee to remain hopeful during a difficult divorce or child custody battle.

Chapter Eleven

CONTROL VERSUS INFLUENCE

There's this beast I contend with on a daily basis. It rears its ugly head in an attempt to make me believe a lie. The lie is simple and terrifying: "You're in control. All of this rests on your shoulders. You are 100 percent responsible for it all." It makes my bones tremble to think about it.

I had been working for the family business for several years before I finally wrestled the lie to the ground and began to see the truth. I remember maniacally laughing out loud as I told David, "We don't have control. It's all an illusion!" I think he thought I had finally lost all the sanity I had left on that day, but the revelation was liberating and freeing when it sunk into my soul. Don't get me wrong, I am not saying we aren't responsible for our actions or inactions. Nor am I saying we should do whatever we want and expect good results. Yes, there are consequences for our actions, but ultimately, we don't hold the power we think we hold. We can't absolutely control who spends money on our products or services, how much people donate to our cause, or how our team members and clients behave. We can't control the economy, and we definitely can't control the weather. See chapter three if you need a reminder of the last one. #floodpocalypse

11 LEADING WITH JESUS

Let's break down the factors beyond our control. First, let's talk about the people under our authority. I asked a good friend of mine what was hardest for her when it came to leading the people in her charge. Her response, "Wanting to control their free will. You cannot make anyone do anything. They have to choose to make the right decisions, work while on the clock, be nice to customers, and complete the daily tasks I pay them to complete. But that's why God gave them free will, so they can choose, on their own, what to do in a situation."

It can be so hard to allow people to choose, but God allows us to choose, so why would we try and control those around us? Sure, we have to have accountability and policies and procedures, but ultimately, the choice is not ours to make regarding whether people follow instructions or not. Sure, our team members or family members can make the wrong choices leading to termination or bad results, but the choice is in their hands.

David and I do not like to be micromanagers. We like to set people in motion with the right tools and resources to get the job done and allow them to do their thing. Some people can handle that sort of freedom, but others can't. Each team is different, and each industry is different. There's no one-size-fits-all approach to leading and managing. I have been frustrated a number of times by reading books that didn't seem to address the concerns of small businesses. Big corporations are set up differently and likewise experience a different set of problems. A lot of books make it seem like things should run like a well-oiled machine if you're a good leader. In a perfect world, maybe so. If you have enough money and manpower, I believe it is possible. Sometimes you don't have either, and you're left feeling powerless. Regardless of all that, or whether we are small or large, none of us are in absolute control. Although as Christians, we know who is. Proverbs 16:9 tells us, *"A man's heart plans his way, but the Lord directs his steps."*

Let's take a look at the story of Ruth and Naomi. Both of these ladies lost husbands and children. I'm sure it is not what they had planned for their lives. I am sure they planned to live happily ever after. Naomi encouraged Ruth, her daughter-in-law, to return to her family, but Ruth had free will. She had the choice to stay with her mother-in-law and help her or to leave her alone. Naomi didn't plan for Ruth to join her as she traveled to her relatives house, but Ruth went anyway. The Lord was directing her steps.

Ruth chose not to give up on God in the face of adversity. She earned favor with Boaz, Naomi's relative, and he invited her to stay in his fields. Ruth soon married Boaz, the wealthy landowner, and ultimately, she gave birth to the father of David. The best time for God to show up and do something amazing in our lives is when we finally give up control and realize we are in His hands.

One of the most quoted verses in the entire Bible is found in Jeremiah. *"For I know the thoughts I think toward you, says the Lord, thoughts of peace and not of evil, to give you a future and a hope. Then you will call upon Me and go and pray to Me, and I will listen to you. And you will seek Me and find Me, when you search for Me with all of your heart"* (Jeremiah. 29:11-13). This verse can alleviate the pressure we put on ourselves to get it all right and do it all in perfect cadence. It seems most people only focus on the eleventh verse, *"to give you a future and a hope,"* and they skip over the part where we have to pray and seek God. Matthew also tells us, *"But seek first the kingdom of God and his righteousness, and all of these things will be added to you"* (Matthew 6:33). I have seen a lot of people giving God credit, in a negative way, for things He may not have done. For example, when someone loses a job for not showing up to work on time, but then says God took the job away to bring him something better. Yes, God may bring the person a better job, but it's also true that a person who doesn't show up for work on time must face the consequences. As a leader, you can't control your team by waking them, dressing them, feeding them breakfast and then driving them

11 LEADING WITH JESUS

to work every day. Although, some people would allow you to do so if you're willing.

INFLUENCE

While you may never have total control, you can attain influence. Jesus is the greatest influencer of all time, and He gives you an example of what it means to influence others. He influenced an entire world in His short time on earth. He tells us in John 14:6, *"I am the way, the truth, and the life. No one comes to the Father except through me."* You have to allow Jesus to wrap you up in the Truth, so you can share it with the people in your world. When you develop credibility with your team members and community by not only talking the talk but walking out your faith, you gain influence in their lives. The very voice you use to promote Jesus, begins to carry more weight. After our store flooded, our team watched how we carried ourselves. They paid attention to our attitudes, and during this trial, we were able to gain influence in their lives. They saw us come to work in old clothes, rain boots, and baseball caps pushing mops and handling the gross stuff.

It is your responsibility, not your pastor's or well known authors, to seek out the heart of God by reading and studying His word on a personal level. In order to influence others for Christ, you don't have to be a theologian, but you do need to be a student eager to learn more and more, so you can share what God is doing in and through you. It's powerful to share your journey with the Lord with those around you. You have to allow God to transform your heart, mind and life. As you do, your testimony becomes a powerful faith-building tool.

David and I didn't have to think about how we were going to act in our wet circumstances, because we were already prayed up and fueled on God's Word. Our reaction to the flooding was a visible showing of who we were on the inside. People want to see who you

CONTROL VERSUS INFLUENCE 11

are on the inside. Our outward reactions can influence the world for Jesus or turn them off to Jesus.

I remember the first time I shared the gospel with a team member. She believed in Jesus, but had not surrendered her life to the Lord. It didn't happen overnight. It was a slow process of connecting with her, showing her God's love for her, and speaking truth into her situation. I had to earn her trust and respect before she would consider listening to my message of hope and deliverance. It took time and patience. You're not going to change anyone's mind by aggressively screaming at them or by telling them they are bound for hell fire and brimstone.

I hold fast to the belief that although I have to do my part and be obedient to God, none of our success is based on what I have done. God has given us our talents and abilities. He has made it all possible and He should receive all the glory. My gifts are given to me from God, and it's up to me to steward them well. As a person who wants to influence others for the kingdom of God, we have to give credit where credit is due. Sometimes our prideful flesh wants us to say, "I did that," or "I made it happen," but our submitted hearts should shout, "It was all God! Give Him the glory. I am nothing without Him." That's exactly my heart's cry post flood. We are solely dependent on Him for our provisions and for making a way when there doesn't seem to be a way. When we begin to share the miracles we have experienced while under God's care, people will begin to take notice and wonder in amazement at the goodness of Jesus. And that's the goal. We need people to be in wonder of Jesus and not in wonder and awe of us. My prayer many times has been, "God, magnify your presence in my life. Get me out of the way and make Yourself known."

In a world grabbing for your attention and willing hands, it's important to realize that just because you can do something that doesn't mean you should. Christ should be our ultimate focus if we want to influence our family, friends, and workplace for Him. It's easy to fall into the belief that as long as it's for God's glory, it has to be good for you, too. However, you have to be careful that you do not overtax yourself, causing more harm than good to your wellbeing, family, and ministry. God should be your priority, and signing too many volunteer sheets at the church can leave you breathless and burned out. It's hard to influence well when we are exhausted or maybe even bitter due to all of our commitments.

Lukewarm won't cut it, friends. *"So I will spit you out of my mouth, because you are only warm and not hot or cold"* (Revelation 3:16). Once I had someone tell me, "I'm not that religious. I believe in God, and I have been saved, but I just don't really get into it." The world doesn't notice us when we are lukewarm. We look too much like the world when we are warm. In order to influence others, we must be on fire for God in our speech, behavior, leadership style and daily walk.

GOD'S AUTHORITY

It's important you humble yourself, as a leader, and recognize you are also under an authority. Obviously, you are under God's authority, but you are also under the authority of your pastor. Hebrews 13:17 tells us, *"Obey your leaders and submit to them, for they are keeping watch over your souls, as those who will have to give an account. Let them do this with joy and not with groaning, for that would be of no advantage to you."* In order to be a good influence, you need good influences. Seeking the Lord and godly counsel in your leadership role helps ensure you remain on the right path. Godly counsel can come in many different forms. It's up to you to use discernment in deciding whose counsel you will take.

In addition to seeking wise counsel, you have to freely and unashamedly admit you are an imperfect person who makes mistakes. Owning up to your mistakes will increase your sphere of influence, especially when you take corrective action. I have said I'm sorry to team members when goals weren't communicated effectively.

It can be hard to admit when I am wrong, but in all of my experience team members are more forgiving when I am straightforward and transparent, which leads to more influence in their lives. There's never a time when we, as a leader, have arrived. It's a daily journey where we learn day by day what works and what doesn't. Leaders must be consistent. Team members should know what to expect from a good leader. They should be able to anticipate their thoughts and make decisions in their absence, because the leader has taught them well.

Great leaders develop more leaders. This process can be long and painful, but it is worth it. I remember when I first heard of the concept of developing leaders, I looked around and didn't see as many leaders on my team as I wanted to see. As I began to train people to lead, over time, I saw my team become more independent, more focused on goals, and ready to take on new levels of responsibilities. Your goal, as a leader, is to duplicate yourself in others so that the work can be divided and have a bigger impact. The apostle Paul said, *"Imitate me as I imitate Christ"* (1 Corinthians 11:1).

THE STORY OF JETHRO

In the book of Exodus, Jethro, Moses' father-in-law, pays Moses a visit after hearing about all God had done for him and the people of Israel. Moses and Jethro then spent time talking inside the tent about all of the good things God had done. The next day, Jethro watches from morning until night while Moses settles disputes amongst the people. When Moses finally finished for the day, Jethro asks, *"What is this that you are doing for the people? Why do you sit alone, and all of the people stand around you from morning till evening"* (Exodus 18:14)? I'm sure Jethro, being older and wiser, saw it all as a ridiculous burden. Moses then explains to his father-in-law that he has to do it because the people come to him and inquire of him all day. Jethro replied, *"What you are doing is not good. You and the people*

11 LEADING WITH JESUS

with you will certainly wear yourselves out, for the work is too heavy for you. You are not able to do it alone" (Exodus 18:17-18). I can relate to Moses so much in my daily walk in leadership. I want to be able to answer all the questions and solve all of the problems. A lot of leaders have the mentality, "If I want it done right, I have to do it myself." While that statement is true sometimes, you can't live your life like that and experience peace and rest. You have to be able to put the reins of control down and allow your employees to pick them up, so they can practice how to lead. In some cases, you have to create a vacuum and stop enabling employees by picking up their slack. There comes a point when they have to take responsibility. At the end of the story, Jethro tells Moses to make sure the people know the laws and what is expected. Then, he says Moses needs to, *"look for able men from all the people, men who fear God, who are trustworthy and hate a bribe, and place such men over the people as chiefs of thousands, of hundreds, of fifties, and of tens"* (Exodus 18:20-21).

This bible passage marks the advent of delegation and management teams. Small matters were to be decided by managers and big matters were to be brought to Moses (Exodus 18:22). Jethro's advice is a wise example to follow. It's important to empower team members and managers to handle day-to-day matters.

Sometimes empowerment is sending your managers to off-site training or offering an incentive if they read a book on a leadership topic you choose. We have offered staff members $50 to read a book we chose and discuss what they learned from the book with us. Other times, role playing works well. I have sat down with management team members and role-played situations so he/she could learn how to handle those situations within their departments. While I gain influence in the lives of my managers, they, in turn, gain influence with members under their care.

Most leadership is learning by doing. You have to figure out what works best for you and your team. I wish I could come up with a

CONTROL VERSUS INFLUENCE

formula that worked every single time in every situation, but that's impossible. However, there is one strategy that works every time — taking my requests to the Lord in prayer, allowing Him to speak into each situation, and giving up my illusion of control.

I had never felt so out of control of our business as I did when the flood consumed much of it. There was nothing I could do to make it better overnight. I had to completely hand it all over to the Lord and say, "You gave all of this to us, and you have the power to take it all away." I trusted He would work it all out for our good. As I write these words, we aren't on the other side of the flood situation, yet. We are still walking it out daily. Our main location is closed for renovations while we operate from a temporary location. We still have many things to decide. Will we keep the second location when we finish renovating the first location? What changes will be made to help prevent this from happening to us again? We don't have all of the answers. There are times when bad things have happened and I have wracked my brain for a solution. I am always looking for a strategic plan to fix whatever is broken. I have friends who bring me problems, and they just want to be heard, but my mind starts racing and looking for the answer. What I should do instead is take all these problems to the Ultimate Troubleshooter. While I didn't have control after the flood, I had a place of influence. A local news station saw my live Facebook video and took note of my calmness and positive attitude while I waded through two to four feet of water inside our dark and wet business. People from the community commented on how we were handling the dismal circumstances in a way that honored the Lord. We chose to be a light during a time when it would have been easy to sit in the dark and camp in our despair. We chose to look at the flood as an opportunity to show our community who God is to us and how He sets us apart, puts our feet upon the Rock, and protects us even when our earthly eyes show a different story.

11 LEADING WITH JESUS

FAITH BUILDERS

As I mentioned earlier, our testimony can help build the faith of others, but it can also build our own faith. Several years of my life were filled with various challenges. My health was attacked, my children were attacked, my marriage was attacked, and my business was attacked. I lost loved ones and experienced deep heartache. I took time to write down a list of the attacks. Thankfully, beside each attack, including the flood, I was able to write a "but God" statement. God healed. God redeemed and restored. God provided a way out when there was no way. As I read each of the times God rescued me and my family, I started to glean more hope for my current situation. Now, when I am feeling helpless or hopeless, I can look at the list and be reminded of what God has done and have faith in what He will do. *"You are the salt of the earth; but if the salt loses its flavor, how shall it be seasoned? It is then good for nothing but to be thrown out and trampled underfoot by men"* (Matthew 5:13). During the good times, it's easy to retain the salt, flavorful and full of goodness. But when tragedy strikes, and everyone is watching, how will we react? Matthew goes on to say, *"You are the light of the world. A city that is set on a hill cannot be hidden. Nor do they light a lamp and put it under a basket, but on a lampstand, and it gives light to all who are in the house. Let your light so shine before men, that they may see your good works and glorify your Father in heaven"* (Matthew 5:14-16).

We have a choice whether we are a positive influence or a negative influence on those around us. Whether we have control or not, we have influence when we are in a place of leadership. It's up to us how we use the influence we have been granted.

EXERCISE

1. Think about the influence you have with your coworkers, family and

team. What could you do to gain more influence for God in the lives of those around you?

2. How much control do you think you have over your life and in your workplace?

3. Be honest. Who do you believe has control over your business? Allow God to be the pilot of your organization. Be in tune with the Holy Spirit so you don't miss His voice when He speaks to your spirit to guide your steps.

Chapter Twelve

WORK LIFE BALANCE: IT THAT A REAL THING?

Both my husband and I have always been hard workers. We are borderline workaholics. My Dad always worked multiple jobs, and my Momma never sat down. When she wasn't working outside of the home, she was working inside of our home cleaning, cooking and serving us. My husband also watched his parents work hours upon hours trying to keep the doors of their small business open. It's in our nature to want to work all the time, to accomplish as much as possible, and to take on loads of responsibility, not just at our day jobs but in our community and church.

My Dad was an auto body repairman. He was a master dent removing, sanding, Bondo spreading, paint-spraying machine. His work was always his very best. He was a perfectionist, always wanting things to be just so. I watched him work on the same spot for a week at a time trying to make sure the body of the car was as smooth as possible. He was well known in our town as one of the best in the business. He took pride in his work.

In the hot summer month of August 1996, I turned sweet 16. My Daddy surprised me with a car that I did not appreciate as I should have. Sure, I was happy to just have wheels, but at the time, I didn't find it as cool as some of my friends' rides. It was not exactly what I wanted since it was seven years old. It was also a four cylinder. I begged daddy for a V6. He laughed and said, "No, you aren't ready for that." I wanted a Camaro. It was my "dream car."

My daddy spent a lot of time visiting junk yards. He had found my car, "the old girl" someplace with a wrecked front end. She only had 60,000 miles on her—something I now appreciate—and the interior looked pristine. My Daddy saw the potential, bought me the car, fixed the front end, and gave it a fresh new coat of maroon paint before presenting it to me — a 1989 Pontiac Sunbird. The headlights flipped up with the press of a button, which was cool at first, but sometime after my first accident, which you'll read about later, the feature didn't work when I turned my lights off. I drove around town cock-eyed — one headlight up and one down.

My Daddy worked two steady jobs my whole life, and three if you count the nights he spent playing music with his band. He had a job at a nearby bicycle manufacturing company, and he worked for himself in his auto body shop as well as for an auto body shop a twenty minute drive from our home. From the time I was born until the time he had an accident that took away his ability to walk, talk and work, he labored hard. How he had time to work on my birthday car, I still don't know.

NOT GOOD AT STOPPING

My Momma and Daddy gave me what they could, and my car truly was good enough for a newly driving 16 year-old. When I began my own family, it didn't take me too long to figure out the sacrifices they were making for me. The fact of the matter is most of us, as teens, don't appreciate the sacrifices our parents make for us until we become a parent or parent-figure ourselves. It's similar to first time leaders. You begin to have a new appreciation for previous

WORK LIFE BALANCE: IS THAT A REAL THING?

supervisors.) I drove my car around a couple of months before I had my first accident. There were three of us in the car. I had driven one of my friend's to her house. I don't even remember why. On our way back, one friend sat in the passenger seat, and one on the console of my car. Do you remember when people sat on the console? How dangerous! How dumb. But we did it. The one perched upon the console was controlling my CD player which was plugged in via my cigarette lighter. I was so cool. We were probably singing, "So, tell me what you want, what you really really want..I wanna, I wanna....." The Spice Girls were the thing.

We were laughing, singing and playing the music entirely too loud, I'm sure. Windows were down, and our hair was blowing in the wind as we traveled down a country road. Even though my car was a four cylinder, I usually drove a little too fast. Sorry, Mom. I'm sure if you're reading this, you already know.

Suddenly, a stop sign popped up out of nowhere. I slammed on my brakes sliding in gravel until my car crossed a lane of traffic and came to rest in a ditch on top of someone's barbed wire fence. Thankfully, no one was coming.

I was completely stuck. My heart raced, and my palms broke out in a sweat. How I wished I could just get in the car and drive out of the ditch with no one being the wiser, but I wasn't going anywhere without some assistance. This happened before cell phones, so we walked to a nearby house, insides shaking. A familiar face came to the door and walked to my car with us. I had to call my Dad using his landline. I remember feeling so sick having to make the call.

Most of the details are a blur, except I remember when my Dad arrived, I said, "My brakes went out." My Dad shot back, "Your brakes don't just go out and then come back on. Gulp. He was smarter than me. I knew lying to my Dad wouldn't work. I really didn't want to lie to him, but I didn't want to disappoint him either. However, I could tell he was terribly disappointed. For me, the look on his face was the worst

12 LEADING WITH JESUS

punishment.

He was simultaneously aggravated and grateful. I knew he was thankful no one was hurt, but my car was damaged: broken headlight, missing hubcap, and a busted front end. All those hours he didn't have to spend fixing up a car I half-appreciated were hanging around my neck like a sign of shame. Ugh. The disappointment. I hated disappointing him.

He hauled my car and all my shame home with him. He ended up repairing my car so it was driveable again, although I had to live with the busted bumper. I didn't blame him.

I never wrecked her again. She had mechanical problems, and he taught me how to fix them. I remember stopping on the side of the highway, popping the hood, and tightening the distributor cap. Dad taught me to always keep the oil changed, and I did. He taught me to keep my car clean, and I did. I did everything he asked of me. When I started college at the University of North Alabama in 1998, I also got a job at Wal-Mart. I was driving back and forth almost every day from my hometown thirty miles away. My Sunbird began to have more and more issues. Since I was making my own money and paying my own car insurance, it was time for a different car.

My Dad had watched me as a full-time student working 25 to 30 hours a week. He watched me keep the oil changed in my car. He watched me keep my car clean. He watched me learn what to do when something went wrong with my car.

We drove to Nelda Stephenson Chevrolet, and he signed a note with me to get a 1997 Camaro with five star wheels. My car had WHEELS, y'all, not just hubcaps. I was so excited. It was emerald green and beautiful.

I still have dreams about this car, dreams that she is still stowed away in a garage for me. Ha! I made every payment on her myself, and the payments were ridiculous. My Momma and Daddy tried to talk me out of it, but I wouldn't listen. After about a year, I ended up totaling my "dream car."

Would you believe it involved another STOP sign? A tree had grown out over it at a two-way stop. I was supposed to stop, but I didn't see the sign. An oncoming car slammed into the side of my car and totaled it. I walked away a little shaken, but completely unharmed. This time, I knew better than to blame it on brake failure. Facepalm. I really didn't think there was a lesson in this story-telling session, but God spoke to me as I typed it out and said, "You've never been good at stopping. If you would have paid attention and stopped, neither wreck would have happened."

Whoa! Profound, Lord.

It's so true. We can be bad at resting. We can be reluctant to slow down and take a breath, guilt free, before we slide off into a ditch or get blindsided by life?

Resting doesn't mean you quit doing what you are supposed to do. It simply means it's important to make time for yourself, time to rest. Take time to embrace your human need for respite. You're not a machine with a distributor cap that just needs tightening, like my first car, so you can keep going. You are a spiritual being with a physical need to slow down so you can be the best version of you.

LEARNING TO REST

Rest and worship are the primary purposes of the Sabbath Day, and yet we find a way to mess it up even when we know what's right. Jesus rested. *"On that day, when evening had come, he said to them, 'Let us go across to the other side.' And leaving the crowd, they took him with them in the boat, just as he was. And other boats were with him. And a great windstorm arose, and the waves were breaking into the boat, so that the boat was already filling. But he was in the stern, asleep on the cushion. And they woke him and said to him, 'Teacher, do you not care that we are perishing?' And he awoke and rebuked*

12 LEADING WITH JESUS

the wind and said to the sea, 'Peace! Be still!' And the wind ceased, and there was a great calm" (Mark 4: 35-38). Jesus loved the people he was ministering to, but he also needed breaks. Seemingly, the people had exhausted him, because it appears Jesus fell asleep pretty quickly on the boat. I know I have been worn myself "slap out" by those around me and passed out in exhaustion at 7:00 p.m. instead of the usual 10 or 10:30 p.m. ("Slap out" is a good southern term, like "dog tired," for those who may not have heard it).

When we examine this passage, we see Jesus left the crowd. If there was a crowd of people surrounding Him, there was work to be done. Jesus saw the value in taking time to escape and rest. I know it can be really hard for me to rest when I know there is work to be done, but if Jesus sets this example for me, it must be a good one. Plus, I don't have life or death situations calling out to me, like Jesus did. People aren't showing up at my business for healing or the casting out of demons. Granted, I would stop what I was doing to help if that happened to be the case. What's amazing is that even though Jesus had people, with compelling reasons, calling out to him, He still experienced guilt free rest. It's so freeing to keep this illustration in mind, especially when your work isn't finished, but you are.

You can also see Jesus resting in Matthew 14:22-25. *"Immediately he made the disciples get into the boat and go before him to the other side, while he dismissed the crowds. And after he had dismissed the crowds, he went up on the mountain by himself to pray. When evening came, he was there alone, but the boat by this time was a long way from the land, beaten by the waves, for the wind was against them. And in the fourth watch of the night he came to them, walking on the sea."*

Again, Jesus dismissed the needy crowd and the disciples. He spent a lot of time with his disciples, but he recognized a need to be totally alone. Jesus spent quality time with the Father. During your quiet time with the Lord, He can guide you on when to work and when to rest. He can answer questions like, "Do I say yes or no to this commitment?"

THE YES GENE

It seems like many of us have a "yes" gene. You know, the gene telling us to agree to everything. Sure, I can do that. Yes, just one more thing. Why not? Pile it on us. We're leaders, we can handle it. Maybe we can handle it, but at what price?

Donald Miller writes about life themes and filtering every decision we make through those themes. Your life themes are what you want to be remembered for when you leave this life. Anytime a non-obligatory or optional task is asked of us, we must filter that request through our life theme. When we say yes to one thing in our lives, we are ultimately saying no to something or someone else. Lysa Terkeurst's, "The Best Yes" delves into this concept. I would encourage you to take some time to read the whole book if you struggle with saying no and feel compelled to do everything asked of you. Saying yes is not a bad thing, but it is a decision we make. A decision which impacts our work-life balance.

An oversimplified example would be me saying, "Sure, I will make fifty cupcakes for the classroom party tomorrow," or "Sure! I can definitely have that fifty page report that I haven't started on your desk by tomorrow." By agreeing to these tasks, I could be saying no to time with my family or to sleeping. The hours spent baking cupcakes or writing reports can take the focus off of our main priorities.

I'm not saying writing the last-minute report or making the cupcakes are bad uses of your time, but I am saying we have to set boundaries to take care of ourselves and those we love. Most of the time, people are going to freely take your time and your talents if you don't learn to say no.

David is notorious for wanting to add "just one more thing" to his already full plate. Since we are in business together, whatever he adds to his plate also gets added to mine. Recently, he had an idea for additional services we could offer to our customers. In theory, the services made sense and were a great idea. However, our plates are already brimming over full with responsibilities. I asked him, "What are you going to take off of your plate so you can add this new venture?" He didn't have an answer. To me, gluttony not only has to do with eating too much actual food, but it has to do with excess in any area. I told him I felt like we were gluttons for work as we try to cram more and more on our plates and ultimately into the belly of our lives. Sometimes, you have to make the decision to trade one thing for another in order to keep your sanity, peace, and joy.

We can't be all things to all people. Sometimes saying yes to others is saying, "No, I won't get any rest," "No, I won't exercise," "No, I won't go to the doctor and get that suspicious area checked." We are sometimes saying no to our mental, physical, spiritual and emotional health.

When we attempt to become superhuman, we are left feeling exhausted, frustrated, overwhelmed and sometimes depressed. While we were recovering our business from the flood, I had to be less involved at my boys' school. I felt bad about it, at first, but I had to cut myself some slack. You have to cut yourself slack, too. If you can't go into a responsibility with a cheerful heart, you may not need to be there. You may be doing too much.

Trying to accept the fact that I have limits and need rest is really hard for me. I don't do a great job of taking care of me. Over time, I have begun to accept that I am not a bad person for saying no to some things in my life. If anything, saying no allows me to concentrate more energy and attention on the people and things that matter the most in my life. What seems like a good opportunity shouldn't always equate to an immediate yes. Distractions often come clothed as good opportunities. Distractions cause us to lose focus on what we are supposed to be doing, and distractions slow us down.

    We've all been burned-out and stressed-out with work. And not just work, but things like parenting a middle school kid or dealing with a friendship on the rocks. The to-do list grows, and the days seem to shrink. However, at some point, I have to learn to turn work off when I leave the building. If I have things I must accomplish at home, I have to make sure I am setting aside a certain amount of time to finish; not just losing myself in my work to the point that I don't notice my husband or my children.

    My car wrecks are such tangible reminders of the importance of paying attention to the spiritual, mental, physical and emotional wreck that's coming if we don't take time to stop. I have found my anxiety levels are always highest when I am tired and run down. What seems like something small ends up snowballing into a huge issue, because I am fragile and running on empty. I can usually feel it happening. All of the physical symptoms of anxiety surge through my body. My chest begins to tighten, my head pounds, and my thoughts, like a whirlwind, take over my mind, swirling so quickly I can't seem to gain control of them. Brick by brick, anxiety builds. I begin to feel like I am smothering. I pray just enough to keep from completely feeling like I am losing control.

    Most recently, the anxiety comes when we get a torrential downpour of rain as I don't want to ever walk through another flood in my lifetime. I'm praying for deliverance from the post traumatic stress. I don't want to have sleepless nights when flood warnings surface on the news. Maybe something has happened in your life or business which triggers your anxiety. I finally made the decision to say, "God, if our business floods again, I am taking it as a sign from you that you want us to close shop. So it's up to you what you allow to happen. I will be okay either way, but I will take the hint and move on to something else." Of course, there's a bit of jest in the prayer but also a little truth. Gut level honest is all I know how to be with Him these days. I'm sure He gets a kick out of my silly ways. After all, He created me.

THE BELLY OF ANXIETY

When in a leadership role, the responsibility can become so great we find ourselves in the eye of the storm, the very center of a panic attack. We can find ourselves making our problems bigger than our God. Like fuel to a fire, we can pour on guilt with thoughts like, "I shouldn't feel this way. I know God. I know His plans for me are good." But we can still feel like we are sinking into the abyss of our problems.

I experienced a great deal of anxiety after the torrent of water. I found myself face down, crying out to God often. Even though our woes have nothing to do with eternity, we get worked-up and stressed-out. No matter how small your issues are in the grand scheme of life, they are important to God. If something is important to you, it's important to God. Why else would he keep a record of how many hairs are on your head? In the words of Jesus, *"Why, even the hairs of your head are all numbered. Fear not; you are of more value than many sparrows"* (Luke 12:7). During Jesus' talk, he is telling the people to only fear being cast into hell. He doesn't tell you to fear lack of sales, a bad Google review, a dishonest employee, or even a criminal who steals from you and your family. Even though I know the Word, it can be hard to apply it when the going gets tough.

During one panic attack, I remember asking myself, "Where has my brave heart gone?" I didn't even feel like myself. I felt weak and powerless. I repeated scriptures in my head: *"Be anxious for nothing but in everything by prayer and supplication, with thanksgiving, let your requests be made to God"* (Philippians 4:6). If I dog-eared my bible, Philippians 4:6 would be one of those pages. I often use scripture to talk myself off of the monstrous ledge of anxiety.

I called David, who was working out of town, to say, "I'm struggling today. I'm praying. I'm quoting Bible verses, but I am still struggling." I explained to him the pile of problems I had been dealing with the entire week. One by one, I named the culprit of each anxiety attack. I unleashed my feelings on him like a million arrows. I told him how I knew God was going to take care of me, but I still had to walk through the pain. I compared it to someone deciding to cut my big toe off with a jagged knife. Should that dire situation had happened, I knew I would be okay, but I would still have to go through the pain and anticipation of it being cut off. Wasn't there something to take the edge off and numb the pain?

Poor guy. I'm sure he appreciated being invited to the panic room of my mind. Most of the problems I shared revolved around work and the stress I carried. I was unsure of how to go about casting my cares upon the shoulders of the Lord. I still find myself struggling with this concept since it requires me to give up my sense of control.

During my breakdown, David spoke to me confidently, "It's going to be okay, I promise. God is in control. We just have to trust Him." See, my husband had been doing this leadership gig longer than me, and he knew what anxiety attacks looked like. He was an experienced warrior able to encourage me, telling me things would get better, and I would learn to cope when the enemy attacked. David's words didn't miraculously make all the anxiety dissipate, but his words were helpful in making me feel less alone in my situation. I hope these same words encourage you on your leadership adventure. You have to keep yourself open to encouragement when you're in the dark places. The enemy wants you to close yourself off and become hopeless. One of his greatest tactics is isolation. If he can get you alone, he has a better chance of owning you.

As I opened myself up to edification and truth, I felt my body slightly loosen from its gripping knot, although a bit of adrenaline remained in my veins. I replayed the week's problems in my mind hoping to find some resolve, hoping to figure out why and when and where and how. I continued to pray, sending short prayers through the air like blinking fireflies throughout my day.

I am at God's mercy every minute of every hour of every day. So are you. He holds the stars in the sky, and He holds me and you in every moment before and every moment after anxiety tries to drown us.

Maybe, you are like me, and you get to the end of your rope deciding to take some time for yourself in order to promote balance in your life. You decide to do something you enjoy, but your phone starts ringing with texts regarding the issues you are trying to escape. Your mind is pulled back into the rabbit hole of to-do lists and problem solving. Maybe, you decide to press on with your relaxation day, visiting a local park, and parking your Eno hammock between two tall trees. However, as you nestle in and finally find a sweet spot of rest, your mind races with self-imposed details.

Trying to capture every thought and allow God to calm your heart can be difficult. If we listen quietly, in our moment of need, God often speaks in a gentle whisper saying, "You see these trees holding you up right now? It's taking two of them. Don't try to do things on your own. They didn't get this big and strong overnight. They took time to grow. They've depended on me to give them what they've needed. They've weathered storms, taken beatings from the wind, felt the sunshine, and like you, their roots were under water not too long ago. However, they are still standing, serving my purposes. Are you not worth more than the trees?"

When you think about your daily grind and the problems leading you to a place of anxiety and desperation, what does it look like for you? For me, it's problem after problem, personnel drama, issues beyond my control, feelings of helplessness, exhaustion from long days. It's the fear of failure and the crippling fears that come with questions like, "What if I am not good enough? What if she is mad at me? What if I could have done something better?" I have found perfection to be nothing more than an unattainable illusion – just like control. Deceptive perception calls my name almost convincing me I can obtain this perfect state if I stay up a little later, work a little more, and push myself to extreme limits. The illusion keeps me on the hamster wheel, spinning and spinning. And Satan is satisfied at keeping me dizzy headed.

Anxiety occurs more often on the days I am tired. It's in these times that the pressure is almost more than I can bear, and I find myself saying things like, "I should give up. It's not worth it." Then in a moment of clarity that only God can bring I ask myself, "Why am I trying to bear it all?" God has already told me to cast my burdens on Him (1 Peter 5:7). Sometimes I put forth my best efforts to cast my burdens on Him, but I still try to maintain the illusion of control. Or I will cast my burden on him, temporarily, before picking it back up again. When we profess to believe in God and His goodness and glory, any doubt and uncertainty can lead to feelings of shame and guilt. The shame and guilt add to the anxiety. It's like a cycle.

From the time I called David to confess the state of my well-being, it took me three days to let go and let God, as the old saying goes. Three days!

THE STORY OF JONAH

Remember the story of Jonah? Jonah was an Israelite, who was called by God to be a prophet in Nineveh. He was to go to the people and prophesy regarding its destruction. God had a message he wanted to deliver to the people, and He wanted to use Jonah to deliver the message. Instead of obeying God, Jonah thought he could escape his assignment and sail away. *"Now the word of the Lord came to Jonah the son of Amittai, saying, 'Arise, go to Nineveh, that great city, and call out against it, for their evil has come up before me.' But Jonah rose to flee to Tarshish from the presence of the Lord. He*

12 LEADING WITH JESUS

went down to Joppa and found a ship going to Tarshish. So he paid the fare and went down into it, to go with them to Tarshish, away from the presence of the Lord " (Jonah 1:1-3). I can't imagine running from the very presence of God, but I find myself delaying action when the assignments aren't what I bargained for or requests are overwhelming me. Since Jonah decided to run, *"the Lord prepared a great fish to swallow Jonah. And Jonah was in the belly of the fish for three days and three nights"* (Jonah 1:17).

Three days. Three nights.

Jonah was there for three days before he cried out to God like he needed to in order to receive deliverance. Wow! Isn't it funny how we can be a lot like Jonah?

- We have to be swallowed up by a giant problem for days before we completely surrender to the Lord.
- We sit inside a dark belly of problems surrounded by unsavory smells of defeat. We shut down, and we stop being grateful.
- We hold fast to stubborn ideas and thoughts that tell us we are capable of getting our own selves out of what we have gotten ourselves into. The slime and muck clings to our well-meaning skin.
- We are busy, overwhelmed and completely weary. Little things become big things. Things we could have normally wiped off with a prayer and scripture reading quickly begin to stick to us. The hardness and the grit of the world grasps at our throats cutting off our oxygen until our bodies have a physical reaction to the emotional and spiritual stress. And we panic.

Before we know it, we find ourselves sitting in the belly of the big fish called anxiety. One firefly prayer leads to the next and the next until there is just enough light to give us hope. We breathe a little deeper, finally able to surrender to God. We find strength each time we whisper the name, "Jesus."

And just like Jonah, we are able to say, *"When my soul fainted within me, I remembered the Lord; And my prayer went up to You, Into Your holy temple"* (Jonah 2:7).

Sweet deliverance arrives. *"So the Lord spoke to the fish, and it vomited Jonah on to the dry land"* (Jonah 2:10).

The Bible doesn't say Jonah was blown through the blowhole of the giant fish or the giant fish returned Jonah to dry land. It says, *"it vomited Jonah onto dry land."* Vomit is ugly, messy, foul and repulsive. Your deliverance can be ugly, messy, foul and repulsive.

God is your deliverer. You don't get to choose how God delivers you. It's not always the way you envisioned, and you aren't always delivered how you want to be, but you can be delivered. You must cry out to Him sooner when you feel stress creeping in. You have to be proactive, immersing yourself in His Word and worshipping Him even when you don't feel like you have the energy or the time. This may involve the help of a professional counselor. There is no shame in asking for help. It can be so easy to phone or text a friend when you are stressed to the max. Talking things out with other people can be very therapeutic. Our first step when dealing with massive stress and anxiety should be taking it to God. He is the one who should hear from us first. But it can also be wise to seek the counsel of His people.

GOD IS ALL WE NEED WHEN HE'S ALL WE HAVE

Not long ago, I found myself experimenting with a problem I had. I didn't tell anyone in my circle I was having this problem and the anxiety which ensued. I simply took it to the Lord in prayer. One week, I was struggling particularly hard, and I messaged my best friend asking if we could meet up to talk. She is the kind of friend who will make time for me, but she wasn't able to see me that week. I drove myself to a nearby river, strung my hammock between two trees and prayed. Days and weeks passed with me only communicating with the

Lord about my dilemma. When the Lord is all you have, you'll find the Lord is all you need.

Slowly, but surely, peace filled my heart and mind about the situation. I felt better than I had in awhile. I realized there was something substantial happening inside of me. I was growing emotionally and spiritually because I only had the Lord to help me, and He didn't fail me. I chose to make my problem personal with God and increase intimacy with Him by only sharing my heart with Him. Taking time to separate from your workplace in order to push the reset button is so hard, yet so important. We have to trust God in the going and in the coming. When we take a break to find respite, we have to know He is in control and won't let it all crumble because we have stopped to praise Him and soak in His goodness.

We have to put our organizations and businesses in His hands. In the words of St. Augustine, "Pray as though everything depended on God. Work as though everything depended on you."

Usually, when I look for the root of strangling anxiety, it's a lack of taking my every need to the Lord. I try to shoulder it all myself. I've overfilled my plate. I am not carving out quiet time with the Lord, and every moment is filled with external stimuli. Multiple days of that will easily swallow us up.

In our pursuit of a work-life balance, God is inviting us to sit with Him, spend time with Him, talk to and listen to Him. He needs us to listen carefully so we can hear His plan more clearly. Sometimes we need to cut off the chatter with other people, so we know the voice we are hearing is His and not that of a well-meaning advisor or friend. We can't be satisfied with just posting the verse of the day on our social media accounts (which I love by the way) we have to bask in His presence. We have to spend more time in His word so our souls can rest.

He wants us to turn our pockets inside out and give Him everything we are trying to carry. Every care. Every worry. Every need.

Every thing. Only with open hands can we welcome true deliverance. It is then that we find our feet back on dry land, our breathing steady, and our hearts lighter from receiving His peace.

It's so important that we take time to truly rest, and it's equally important we have people on our team and in our lives who hold us accountable and tell us when enough is enough. David has sent me home from work several times, because he could sense my stress levels rising, and he knew I needed to remove myself from the people and the situation. He handles the day to day pressure better than I do, but it slowly begins to wear him down. Before he knows it, he can be a different person not exhibiting the fruits of the spirit to those around him. And it's up to me to call his demeanor to his attention so he can begin to intentionally make adjustments. Getting away from the crazy can bring us a fresh perspective. We need team members who can also encourage us to rest. While taking a short trip with a friend, I began texting my manager a couple of questions. She politely told me to turn off my phone and enjoy the sunshine. I was thankful for her encouragement. During one particularly stressful time, one of our team members, who knew the joys of business ownership, said, "You two need to get out of here. I will be here tomorrow to take care of things. I want y'all to get some rest." In fact, she threatened to kick us out of the door if we did show up the next day. I was thankful for her firm love.

God gave us the Sabbath day as a gift. He didn't order us to rest on the seventh day just because He wanted to boss us around. He knew we would need this day to rest, and He knew a lot of us would have to be commanded to rest in order to actually do it. If we aren't careful, we can dishonor the Sabbath and find ourselves working seven days a week without taking a break. In all honesty, there will always be one more thing we could be doing, but rest should be on our to do lists, as well. Our bodies, minds, emotions and spirits need at least one day a week for self-care. We can't feel guilty about

12 LEADING WITH JESUS

resting. It's irresponsible of you to not rest, as you are not able to give your best to your family, friends, or your team.

If you are reading this and feeling overwhelmed, overworked, tired, run down and defeated, my hope is you will make time for guilt-free rest. Unclench your jaws. Relax your shoulders. Stop making a fist. Let go of the tension. Do something you enjoy. Love on your family. Rest. Seriously, everyone wins. You win, your family wins, your team members win, and your business wins.

EXERCISE

1. What's the longest amount of time you have gone without doing any work? If you are working seven days a week most weeks, it's time to step back and rethink your schedule. We are less effective when we are overworked.

2. When can you make time for rest? Think about your upcoming year. Go ahead and plan a respite now and stick to your plan to go. Realize that by making time for yourself to recharge, you will be a better parent, a better spouse, and a better leader.

3. What relationships in your world have struggled because of the amount of time you spend working? Make time to rest and repair these relationships.

Chapter Thirteen

GOD'S PROTECTION

    Through various trials in leadership and in other areas of my life, God has drawn me near to Him and His heart, teaching me His ways, binding up my wounds, helping me to make right my wrongs, making a way when there is no way, and giving me a hope-filled purpose. No matter what the dreams and desires of my heart may be from day to day, I have to bring those dreams and desires to the throne of my Father. I have to offer them up to Him asking Him to have His way. The same Father who knitted me together in my mother's womb and formed my innermost parts has planted in me seeds of purpose. God's love for us is extravagant. When I consider that He sacrificed His only Son, so that we may live, I am overwhelmed with gratitude for the precious blood of Jesus. I am also in awe of the God of the universe, who gave His all just to be near me. We must never underestimate the power He holds and the power He gives us because we are His sons and daughters. It's the power we receive through the stripes Jesus suffered on the cross.

    Sometimes I feel like I don't have a wonderful, heart-wrenching testimony that will help lead someone to give their life to God. I have never been addicted to drugs, raped, sexually molested or in jail.

13 LEADING WITH JESUS

Thank you, God! So I asked God, "What is my story?" He answered with, "All of those things could have happened to you." I began thinking about a variety of things I have lived through in my life. God reminded me of all the times He protected me from the plan of the enemy. There were many events flashing through my mind I had forgotten about. During these times, devastating things could have happened to me, even death, but God had His mighty hand upon my life. Remembering these times helps me to trust God to protect me in the future.

While I was praying, I saw God in the details, pushing back the enemy, since the day I was born. When I was dying from a high fever and a seizure at 18 months old, I saw Him with me. When I was a child and had a penny lodged in my esophagus, He kept me alive. He protected me from instances where my childhood innocence could have been taken away from me. His hand was on me, protecting my heart, when I was a kid experimenting with a Ouija board at a friend's house.

He kept me safe at 16 when I drove my car too fast, or rode with a friend who did. He protected me when I totaled my car. He protected my heart from boys who were up to no good. He held me when my heart was breaking as I watched my parents have some horrific fights due to my Dad's alcoholism. He was my strength and gave me His peace, which surpasses understanding, when my earthly daddy had a car accident, and then again when he passed away as I held his hand. I see God's hand over my marriage. During a time I was ready to quit, He reminded me that the promise I made was first and foremost to Him, and then to my husband.

I remember two scary cesarean sections, including one that was an emergency, when my boys were born. He was with me in Haiti when I went on my first mission trip and climbed a mountain with only a few other team members to share the gospel of Jesus with people. I remember during the recession when we weren't sure how

GOD'S PROTECTION 13

our business would survive the difficult times, God always made a way. I think about the times critical personnel left quickly and without warning. None of us were sure how we would have enough help and hands to do all that needed to be done, but God always sent the right people at the right time. I remember the great flood, which came close to wiping us out, and I can't help but see Him working everything out for our good and His glory, because He loves us. We love Him and are so grateful He is the ultimate leader in our lives. He is all over my story. He's all over yours, as well. Perhaps you can think of times in your life where you've witnessed His invisible hands directing your paths. Times you weren't aware of where your protection or provision came from, but it came. Ultimately, all of these events point to God. There have been many times in my life I wasn't walking with God, but He was walking with me. His faithfulness to us doesn't depend on our faithfulness to Him. He pursues me and my heart. He pursues you, too. I can hear him telling the enemy, "Back off, she belongs to me. I have great plans for her to do my work." My life could have gone in so many different directions, but God was always there covering me with His wings.

If you need reminding of the protection you have in God, here are a few of my favorite verses:

- "He shall cover thee with his feathers, and under his wings shalt thou trust: his truth shall be thy shield and buckler. Thou shalt not be afraid for the terror by night; nor for the arrow that flieth by day." — Psalm 91:4 (KJV)

- "But the Lord is faithful. He will establish you and guard you against the evil one." — 2 Thessalonians 3:3

- "Let us hold fast the confession of our hope without wavering, for he who promised is faithful." — Hebrews 10:23

13 LEADING WITH JESUS

HE NEVER FORSAKES US

He hears your prayers. When you feel like you are losing as a leader, He is there. When you feel like all hope is gone, He is there. When you feel you have been abused or forgotten, He is there. He wants success for you. He wants you to fulfill His Great Commission to, *"Go unto all the world and share the gospel"* (Matthew 28:19). He will stop at nothing to help you share His goodness and love with those around you.

When the bills mount up, the people on your team are dissatisfied with your decisions, and bad news is blasting you from every side, God fights on your behalf. He knows the potential of our hearts even when we are far from Him. His grace and mercy rushes like rolling water to cover our shortcomings, our sins, and our lack of faith. Even though I have witnessed God's miracles many times in my life, I still have to pray, "Lord, give me more faith." I can't always muster up enough on my own.

God knew before I did that I would praise His name once He got me on the other side of whatever I was walking through. According to FEMA, forty to sixty percent of businesses never reopen their doors after a natural disaster. The fact we were able to reopen our doors after the flood is recorded in my mind as another miracle. Most people are intrigued by the story, because, whether they realize it or not, they sense something unnatural happened during that time period.

If you are asking the Lord to use you for His kingdom, you have to be prepared for the battles you will fight, while simultaneously remembering you never fight alone. We must have the courage and the confidence of David as he raced toward Goliath with five smooth stones, a slingshot and God's protection. The great Martin Luther King, Jr. was close to giving up on his mission to bring equality to all mankind when he had a Holy Spirit moment at his kitchen table, over a cup of coffee, where the Spirit confirmed he was fighting the

GOD'S PROTECTION 13

good fight for civil rights and encouraged him to continue to seek righteousness, truth, and justice.

There will be many times as you strive to lead for Jesus that you feel weak, exhausted and weary. Your body will hurt. Your mind will struggle to concentrate on reading scriptures. Your mouth will be at a loss for words to pray. It's in these spiritual moanings that God has the ability to hear us.

"Likewise the Spirit helps us in our weakness. For we do not know what to pray for as we ought, but the Spirit himself intercedes for us with groanings too deep for words. And he who searches hearts knows what is the mind of the Spirit, because the Spirit intercedes for the saints according to the will of God" (Romans 8:26-27). Sometimes all we can do is cry. The good news is, God understands tears. He can interpret your tears just as well as he can interpret your words.

"You keep track of all my sorrows. You have collected all my tears in your bottle. You have recorded each one in your book" (Psalm 56:8). Sometimes I wonder just how big my bottle of tears must be. I know I have cried a lot in my lifetime, and I know there will be more in the future. Never underestimate how much God cares for you. There's no problem too small to take to Him. Luke 12:17 tells us, *"Why, even the hairs on your head are all numbered. Fear not; you are of more value than many sparrows."* If He takes the time to number the hairs on our heads, He is interested in whatever concerns us. Growing up, my Momma would often clean house or ride in the car singing, "His eye is on the sparrow, and I know He's watching me." We can be sure God values us and our lives.

Even though we aren't required or capable of repaying God for His goodness through our deeds, I can't help but believe I owe Him nothing less than my best praise and worship. Worship comes in the form of using our gifts and talents to the best of our abilities. A lot of people consider worship as only the singing of songs or the playing of musical instruments, but it can come while painting, teaching, creating

13 LEADING WITH JESUS

marketing campaigns, volunteering, doctoring patients, completing expense reports or presenting cases in court. We should worship well, because He has given us victory through Jesus! His protection, then and now, is overwhelming and humbling. It's something to put our praises on.

We have to trust Him to be near us during the storms we experience in our ministries and marketplaces. It's not a matter of if, but when the storms come. It's during those times we have to make sure we put on the full armor of God.

A common misconception people have is, "if this is where God wants me to be, it will be easy." Nope, this is not the case. He calls us into the difficult and into the uncomfortable. Take a look at the lives of David, Paul and especially Jesus.

If your job as a leader, parent, or spouse isn't easy, it doesn't mean that's not God's place for you for a season. If your marriage is struggling, it doesn't mean God won't bless you in the heartache. If your child is having a difficult time at school, it could still be the place God calls him/her to be. If finances seem tough at work, it doesn't mean you should close the doors on your business or your dreams. When you're on God's path to your promised land, the enemy will come against you in monumental ways. 2 Corinthians 4:8-10 says, *"We are afflicted in every way, but not crushed; perplexed, but not driven to despair; persecuted, but not forsaken; struck down, but not destroyed; always carrying in the body the death of Jesus, so that the life of Jesus may also be manifested in our bodies."* I love every part of this comforting verse. It carries hope and an answer for each feeling we may be experiencing.

"After you have suffered a little while, the God of all grace, who has called you to his eternal glory in Christ, will himself restore, confirm, strengthen and establish you" (1 Peter 5:10).

God is in the struggle, chaos and mess creating order and beauty, and weaving together His grand master plan that is bigger than what we can comprehend for those of us who love and trust Him (Romans 8:28). His plan is to develop your character and bless His kingdom. In the end, learning to totally depend on the Lord is a gift. It's more important than how your business fairs. As a believer, your suffering is never in vain with God. Paul confirms this in his second letter to the Corinthians.

"Praise be to the God and Father of our Lord Jesus Christ, the Father of compassion and the God of all comfort, who comforts us in all our troubles, so that we can comfort those in any trouble with the comfort we ourselves receive from God. For just as we share abundantly in the sufferings of Christ, so also our comfort abounds through Christ" (2 Corinthians 1:3-5).

You may be the light someone needs right where you are planted. Don't give up when it's hard. Be so attuned to His voice that you know when it's time to move into His will and His next place for you. Go from glory to glory.

GOD FIGHTS FOR YOU

In the natural, fighting stirs up emotions of fear, hopelessness, panic and conflict. Whether it's an actual fight with a person, an internal battle related to finances, employee dramas, or a big decision to make, we have to speak to God about the fights we face. Remember Moses' words to the children of Israel, *"The Lord will fight for you; you need only be still"* (Exodus 14:14).

Usually when someone is fighting for you, the person is near. I believe it's the same for God. He is near you when He is fighting for you. There are times God calls for your stillness. He doesn't want you to defend yourself, to reply to the negative Facebook comments, to call your sister out for the lies she spoke against you, or to shout it from the rooftops how you have been wronged. He asks us to simply put on the armor He provides.

13 LEADING WITH JESUS

"Finally, be strong in the Lord and in the strength of his might. Put on the whole armor of God, that you may be able to stand against the schemes of the devil. For we do not wrestle against flesh and blood, but against the rulers, against the authorities, against the cosmic powers over this present darkness, against the spiritual forces of evil in the heavenly places. Therefore take up the whole armor of God, that you may be able to withstand in the evil day, and having done all, to stand firm. Stand therefore, having fastened on the belt of truth, and having put on the breastplate of righteousness, and, as shoes for your feet, having put on the readiness given by the gospel of peace. In all circumstances take up the shield of faith, with which you can extinguish all the flaming darts of the evil one; and take the helmet of salvation, and the sword of the Spirit, which is the word of God, praying at all times in the Spirit, with all prayer and supplication. To that end, keep alert with perseverance, making supplication for all the saints" (Ephesians 6:10-18).

If we clothe ourselves in this armor, we are protected. We don't have to worry about the future or what tomorrow holds, because we know who holds tomorrow. So what does the full armor of God really look like?

Helmet of Salvation — Salvation is our deliverance from sin and its consequences. Jesus died so that you could live. You have to remember that in every situation. No matter what you have done in the past, He has redeemed your future. I love how salvation is depicted by a helmet. It protects your mind, thoughts and emotions. Remember your home is not on this earth with its problems and challenges. You are just a journeymen passing through, sharing love and Jesus with all those you meet so that they may journey with you to be with your Creator.

Breastplate of Righteousness — Righteousness is the quality of being morally right or justified. Just as a breastplate protects your heart, so does God's righteousness. God gives His righteousness to us because none of us are righteous of our own accord (Romans 3:10-12). *"God made him who had no sin to be sin for us, so that in him we might become the righteousness of God"* (2 Corinthians 5:21). Although no one can never become righteous through his/her own works, if you follow the Word and do what is right, God is able to work on your behalf more easily.

Belt of Truth — Truth is standing on God's Word when the world tries to tell you differently. Like the Truth, a belt holds things together and protects us from exposure. The enemy loves to lie and tell you that you are a nobody or that you aren't usable. He likes to tell you people don't like you and that your financial situation will never get any better. He likes to tell you to give up your leadership gig, because you aren't cut out for it or someone else could do it better. Lies! You must know the Word to stand on its truths, so study it and hide it in your heart.

Shield of Faith — Faith is complete trust in God. Faith is also what protects your whole being from the lies of the enemy. God doesn't do anything halfway, which is why He deserves 100 percent of your trust. You have to know and believe He is in control, and that He will see you home one day. Yes, there will be battles along the way, but those battles build character and endurance. *"Suffering produces endurance, and endurance produces character and character produces hope"* (Romans 5:3-4). All believers have hope, a hope for a better tomorrow and a hope of a glorious homecoming.

Praying in the Spirit —The Spirit is the very essence of who God is. You should talk to Him often and seek His presence and counsel, which always comes with wisdom and power to do whatever God is leading you to do. You should carry Jesus and His Spirit with you wherever you trod. He is your Champion and there is no problem or issue He cannot overcome. Whatever you are currently battling, He has already defeated it on your behalf. If sales aren't where they should be, He knows what you need. If your best associate is leaving, He has someone to fill the position. He goes before you and empowers you to follow God's grand plan step-by-step.

Gospel of Peace — As you walk in the footsteps of Jesus you carry His Gospel and peace wherever you go. The peace that comes from a life of walking with Him should be the covering on your feet. It goes with you. The gospel also protects your steps and guides you. His peace never leaves you. When you feel His peace is missing from your life, press in through prayer and ask Him for it. *"How beautiful upon the mountains are the feet of him who brings good news, who publishes peace, who brings good news of happiness, who publishes salvation, who says to Zion, 'Your God reigns"* (Isaiah 52:7).

I have taken many battles on myself that God intended to fight for me. I have yearned to control situations beyond my control. I can tell you it is one of the most freeing things in the world to say, "Here God, take my mess. It's yours. Fight my battle for me." That is what I do at night when I am feeling pain in my heart from stress and disappointments.

In addition to His Spirit and armor, God also gives us friends to stand with us in our battles. It is important that you break secrecy and allow trustworthy people into your battles. Yes, you must protect your heart, but you should also be open and wise to choose those with whom you can share your heart. You need people who encourage you, speak the Word into you and help you pray through difficult situations. People are a blessing that God often uses to meet our needs. You never know when sharing your battle with someone will help both you and the other person. In the same vein, there will be people you need to remove from your life in order to get to where you're going. People who aren't interested in helping you or who reject correction and God-honoring words from you are like dead weights. Pray for them always, but don't make them a part of your inner circle. Allow God to prune away those who aren't for you. Removing people from your life is one of the many ways God will protect you.

GOD'S PROTECTION 13

"Be still and know that I am God" is found in Psalm 46:10. It's not only a verse that looks good on wall art in our homes or on a t-shirt, it's an important weapon used to defeat the enemy. Believers have the choice to put on the full armor and a choice to lay down their burdens. You must lay down team members who are challenging you in a negative way; lay down financial struggles; lay down doubt; lay down striving; and your desire to be in control. Leave these burdens where they belong— at the feet of Jesus. He is the One who can actually do something about it, and the One who has already done something about it. He defeated sin, death and all the garbage we try to lug around when He died on the cross.

"Therefore do not be ashamed of the testimony about our Lord, nor of me his prisoner, but share in suffering for the gospel by the power of God, who saved us and called us to a holy calling, not because of our works but because of his own purpose and grace, which he gave us in Christ Jesus before the ages began, and which now has been manifested through the appearing of our Savior Jesus Christ, who abolished death and brought life and immortality to light through the gospel, for which I was appointed a preacher and apostle and teacher, which is why I suffer as I do" (2 Timothy 2:1-12).

Sharing Jesus with your world will bring about suffering, just as it did for Paul, but it's an honorable suffering that allows you to experience the Lord's goodness on a deeper level in and through your life.

Although God is in control of protecting us, this doesn't mean Christians get to take a backseat and exit the battlefield altogether. *"Anyone who wants to live a godly life, in Christ Jesus, will be persecuted"* (2 Timothy 3:12). We have to battle in prayer and petition the Lord for His will to be done, no matter what that looks like. We have to ask Him to gird us up in His protection and give us strength to handle whatever happens.

What is there to fear? You know the end of the story. You know

13 LEADING WITH JESUS

you have the victory and Jesus wins this thing called life. At the end of the day, you can have confidence in where you are going. Revelation 19:11 says, *"Then I saw heaven opened, and behold, a white horse! The one sitting on it is called Faithful and True, and in righteousness he judges and makes war. His eyes are like a flame of fire, and on his head are many diadems, and he has a name written that no one knows but himself. He is clothed in a robe dipped in blood, and the name by which he is called is The Word of God."*

You shouldn't have confidence in yourself and in your own flesh, but in the King described above. Confidence in yourself will get you into trouble. Look at your track record verses God's. It's not your job to fight alone. You are incapable of winning by yourself. All of your trust should be placed in God who will fight your battles for you if you allow Him to do so.

It's time you stop trying to fight the battle on your own. It's time you put on the full armor of your protection, your Savior and your Redeemer. It's time to trust that your Deliverer will show up, and when he does, HE WILL SET YOU FREE! It's up to you to step out of the shackles and begin living the way He intended. You won't fight forever. One day, you will be able to trade in the whole armor of God, covered in all the battle wounds, blood and tears, for a pure white robe and a jewel-filled crown. Personally, I get a mental picture of myself bowing down at the feet of Jesus laying down my heavy armor as he says, *"Well done, good and faithful servant. You have been faithful over little; I will set you over much"* (Matthew 25:21).

As we strive to have a marketplace ministry or be Jesus to the world, it's natural to be concerned with what people will think or say about us. Some probably think we are crazy. In those moments of human doubt and insecurity, I remind myself of the good, good Father I serve, and I recall all the times He carried me, protected me, and saved me.

If anyone should be ashamed, God should be ashamed of us, but

GOD'S PROTECTION 13

He's not. He is proud of His children, and He wants His best for us. He is always near, and we always have a choice as to whether or not we will shine our light for all to see and share the glory of the Lord with our world or whether we will hide it, keeping it private, afraid to make the great I Am known in our marketplace.

EXERCISE

1. Look back at the pieces of the armor of God. What piece of your armor is weak and could be stronger?

2. What piece of armor do you feel is strongest in your life?

3. What is your decision? Will you bring Jesus into your workplace? Will you take him outside the walls of a church?

Chapter Fourteen

THE WRAP UP: ONE LAST THING. IT'S IMPORTANT

The words written within these pages are based on my experiences as I grow in my faith and continue to wrestle daily with the challenges associated with leading with Jesus. Throughout my journey as a leader, I've changed strategies, tried new things, stopped doing some things, set some boundaries, and made eliminating toxicity a priority in my business and life. Leading with Jesus is a daily choice to choose the next right thing, to keep asking God for guidance and direction, and to accept that when we make mistakes and bad decisions, God is ready and able to turn them around for our good. One Saturday, I was running errands. I had a baby shower and a bridal shower to get to, and my thirteen year old had a birthday party to which he needed a ride. My husband, who is normally helpful in these situations, was home with immobilizing back pain. Getting older can be rough, folks. As I scurried from one event to another on that blustery Saturday, I didn't talk much to God, except to bless my food, but it didn't stop Him from talking to me.

He brought to mind an employee who was struggling with some personal issues. I took the little break I had between running the wheels off my car and drove to our store to check in. It was near

14 LEADING WITH JESUS

closing time when I walked in the door. I greeted the girls working, "How are y'all doing today?" I got the typical, "Good. We were busy there for awhile, but it's slowed down now."

"Great. It looks like it was a decent day," I said as I checked our point of sale system for the day's sales. They nodded their heads in agreement and went on to ask me about the mini vacation I had taken with my family. I gave them a quick run down, and we all laughed about how it was one of those vacations from which you need a vacation when you return. Our hearts were light, except they weren't. I sensed the heaviness in the air.

One of the girls stepped outside to take down some wreaths leaving me alone with the other. The Holy Spirit nudged me, "Ask her how she's really doing."

"Hey," I inched closer to her. "How are you doing?"

"I'm okay," she answered without looking up from the computer screen.

"I mean, like really. How are you?" I pushed.

Tears began to flow down her cheeks as she told me she had been hoping her church community would have asked her how she was doing since she had missed some Sundays due to health issues and the like, but they hadn't. She was hurt in her heart. I spoke a word of encouragement over her, and put my arm around her, allowing her to take a few deep breaths before breaking away. Was it my place to comfort her and allow her to cry into my shoulder for a couple of minutes? Did I have to embrace her and share her pain? No, but this is what leading with Jesus is all about. It was a ministry moment for me, and I view it as no different than working altar call on Sunday morning when someone comes down needing prayer and a person with flesh and bones to hug them close. I kissed her forehead like a mother would a daughter. Obviously, from a human resources perspective, I am not encouraging you to begin kissing your employees, but I have a mothering kind of relationship with this

THE WRAP UP 14

person. She often calls me momma as she doesn't have a connection with her earthly mother.

The Lord gently whispered to my heart, "Take them to dinner." I hesitated making sure I should do so. You have to practice hearing from God, which can take time. It's amazing when you can know you heard from His still small voice. There have been times I am certain I heard straight from the Lord and there were times I questioned whether or not it was just me. I have never heard his voice audibly, but He has spoken to me many times. Sometimes it's a brilliant thought planted in my heart and mind. It's a thought I can't take the credit for thinking, because I'm not that good. There have been times He gave me words to write which flowed so eloquently and beautifully, and I would think, "This is God." Sometimes it's a word of encouragement or confirmation from someone else. The more I hear from Him, the more I become familiar with His voice. He wants to lead alongside you and me. He doesn't want you to merely lead like Jesus would lead, but He wants you to lead with Jesus, to be empowered by His Holy Spirit which lives in you as a believer. Acts 2:38 says, *"And Peter said to them, 'Repent and be baptized every one of you in the name of Jesus Christ for the forgiveness of your sins, and you will receive the gift of the Holy Spirit."* The Bible tells us the Holy Spirit descended upon Jesus like a dove when he was baptized in the Jordan (Luke 3:22). So many people underestimate the power of the Holy Spirit. Maybe you're thinking, "Well, I believe in Jesus, but I don't know about having any power." People can be amazing creations of God who are living powerless lives. They have not tapped into all God has to offer. I don't mean in a mystical, fortune telling kind of way, but in a pure, righteous, life-giving and holy way. God will speak to you, and you can be certain of His voice if you open your spirit and don't allow your heart to harden (Hebrews 3:15). God's Spirit communicates with yours and you hear Him with your spiritual ears. Often He speaks to our hearts by giving us simple instructions and a gentle prompt.

On this particular day, I received simple instructions.

"So, what do you two have planned tonight." They both answered, "Not much."

"Do you want to have dinner?" They both lit up with surprise and excitement, "Yes!" they exclaimed. We balanced the cash drawer, turned off the lights, locked the door, and drove to the nearest Mexican restaurant. Over cheese dip and salsa, we prayed, laughed, and shared our struggles, as we encouraged one another to keep trusting Jesus.

After we left that night, bellies full of tacos and hearts full of connected hope, I got in my car to call my business partner, my husband, and explain to him how wonderful our evening had been together. I remember feeling excitement rush through me as I said, "I think I'm getting it. This is what it's all about. This is marketplace ministry. This is letting your business be your ministry and leading with Jesus outside the walls of a church."

EXERCISE

1. When was the last time you were sure you heard from the Lord? If you can't remember hearing from Him, take time this week to find a quiet place to talk to Him where there are no interruptions. Tell Him, "Lord, I am here willing to listen. What would you like to say to me?"

2. God loves you more than you can ever imagine. He sent His only Son, born of a virgin, to establish a new covenant between Himself and us. In this new covenant, Jesus agreed to pay the price for everyone's sins, yours and mine, by dying a brutal death on the cross. After obeying God by submitting to His will, even unto death, God raised Jesus up by the power of His Holy Spirit. Through Jesus' resurrection, He defeated death and made a way for all of us to be saved from the penalty due to our sins. Have you invited Jesus to be

THE WRAP UP 14

your Lord and Savior? If you've never prayed the prayer of salvation, today is your day!

Father, I admit I don't make the best decisions on my own. I have made mistakes, and I have sinned against you. I ask you to forgive me for my sins and prepare a place for me in heaven. I believe Jesus Christ lived, died and rose from the grave for me, and I accept Him as my Lord and Savior. I accept Him as the ultimate leader of my life. I give my life to Him completely and without reservation. I want Him to lead me for the rest of my life. In Jesus' name I pray, amen.

Author's Notes

Dear Reader,

    I can't begin to thank you enough for taking this journey with me. In the world of leadership, there are no shortcuts or quick fixes. It's a daily trusting of God to provide for our every need. It's looking at His track record in our lives and remembering that He remembers us. As I finish this book, it has been almost a year since the flood attempted to drown our business and our ministry, but God has been faithful to us in this season, more so than I could have ever dreamed or imagined. When we met with our accountant earlier this year, we were told our business was "upside down," and on paper, the outcome looked grim. We worked hard and prayed harder for God's provision, asking for His favor and being grateful for each day the doors of our business remained open. Some days were harder than others as we continued to have new problems arise, but God remained faithful. We ended the year on an amazing note. Although we were closed for a period of time and partially closed for another period of time, we had a good year. God gets every ounce of glory. It was not something we could do on our own. It was a supernatural miracle we will always remember and be grateful for. We ended our year at "net neutral." Basically, it's like having a start-up company again, but we will take it if it means we can continue to serve the Lord the way He wants for us to serve

Him and minister to His people. I encourage you to never doubt God and His plans. No matter how bad the storms may look, He can make it work for your good and His glory. The words in the Bible aren't just words on a page. They are living. They are alive, and they are working to this day for those of us who love the Lord and wish to serve Him and obey Him. He has granted us marvelous grace throughout our journey. It's been so hard to walk out, but we don't walk it out alone. Catastrophes and hard times draw us closer to God to seek His presence and His comfort, and if it takes the hard stuff to keep us close to the Father, it's all worth it. He is worthy to be praised.

I love you all and pray God's richest blessings on each of you.

With Love,

Jen

Jen

SOURCES

16Personalities, Accessed August 2019, http://www.16personalities.com, NERIS Analytics Limited, United Kingdom, 2011-2020

Batterson, Mark, The Cirlce Maker, Grand Rapids, Michigan, Zondervan, 2016.

FEMA, https://www.fema.gov/media-library-data/1441212988001-1aa7fa978c5f999ed088dcaa815cb8cd/3a_BusinessInfographic-1.pdf

Gourley, Bobby, Tactics, Florence, Alabama, 2019

Luther, Martin, 95 Theses, Germany, 1517.

Terkeurst, Lysa, The Best Yes, Nashville, Tennessee, Thomas Nelson Publishers, 2014

www.ingramcontent.com/pod-product-compliance
Lightning Source LLC
Chambersburg PA
CBHW052350220526
45465CB00003BA/1044